TABLE TALK

For Frank Thocker
with best wishes for
years to come. Don't
forget the old ways.

Sidney Saylor Farr

Table Talk

Appalachian
Meals and
Memories

Sidney Saylor Farr

University of Pittsburgh Press
Pittsburgh and London

Published by the University of Pittsburgh Press, Pittsburgh, Pa., 15260
Copyright © 1995, University of Pittsburgh Press
All rights reserved
Manufactured in the United States of America
Printed on acid-free paper

Library of Congress Cataloging-in-Publication Data

Farr, Sidney Saylor, 1932–
    Table talk : Appalachian meals and memories / [compiled by] Sidney Saylor Farr.
      p.   cm.
    Includes index.
    ISBN 0-8229-3785-9 (acid-free paper).—ISBN 0-8229-5533-4 (pbk.)
    1. Cookery—Appalachian Region.   2. Appalachian Region—Social life and
customs.   I. Title.
TX715.F2546   1994
641.59756'8—dc20
                                  94-14553
                                     CIP

A CIP catalogue record for this book is available from the British Library

Eurospan, London

This book is dedicated to my sons,

Dennis Wayne

and

Bruce Alan Lawson

Contents

Acknowledgments

It takes more people than just the author to bring a book to completion, and this book is no exception. I want to thank family, friends, and acquaintances who encouraged me by their interest in the project. My gratitude is extended to the Mellon Foundation, and Loyal Jones who administered the funds at the Appalachian Center of Berea College, for money to travel and interview people and then pay for the tapes to be transcribed. My son Bruce Alan Lawson did editing and proofreading at various stages.

I also want to thank those people through the years who have written or called to ask if I have another book coming out and requested that I take their names and addresses so they could be notified. Last but not least, my heartfelt gratitude to those men and women who permitted me to interview them and so willingly shared their stories and recipes.

Introduction

In any culture people's activities concerning food quite often reflect their social customs and beliefs. The moods and schemes in Appalachia are changing. Microwave ovens, chain grocery stores, cable television, and computers all have invaded the hills. Our ways of cooking and eating are changing. What I hope to convey here, through the eyes of mountain men and women in several southern Appalachian states, is how those changes have affected the different generations. Are the changes good? Is the food as wholesome and pleasing as it was when our grandmothers were young?

I will never forget my shock and dismay when I visited my mother after living in Indianapolis, Indiana, and Asheville, North Carolina. I arrived at Stoney Fork, Kentucky, in the evening. The next morning I awoke with anticipation for Mother's biscuits and gravy, eggs and bacon, along with her boiled coffee. But when we sat down at the table I could not believe my eyes. She had baked canned biscuits and was using instant coffee! "Mother, I never thought I'd see the day you would serve canned biscuits," I said. "I don't go to all the trouble of hot biscuits from scratch," she said, "I just open a can of biscuits and make breakfast the easy way for your brother James and me." I saw her point, of course, but still felt a bit disturbed to have her cooking changed so drastically.

My first cookbook, *More Than Moonshine*, has brought me in

touch with more people than I would have thought possible. There have been numerous letters, telephone calls, and personal comments from people who make it a point to look me up. People like what I told about my family and community, about customs, food ways, and history.

Shortly after *More Than Moonshine* was published, I was invited to speak about mountain food at Sue Bennett College in London, Kentucky, during their annual spring festival. After my presentation people came up to talk and get copies of the book autographed. I noticed a high-school-age boy standing in the back of the room with a book in his hand. When everyone else had left he came up.

"We lost our mother two months ago, and Dad and I have been trying to cook," he said. "Dad read in the newspaper about your book and sent me here to buy one. He said you tell how to make corn bread and cook pinto beans." I assured him there were directions. "Dad went to the store this morning to get beans and cornmeal. He's waiting for me to get home so we can cook some to eat." I autographed the book through my tears, hoping I would not embarrass him because I was crying.

Two years ago I received a letter from a woman who wrote that her grandmother had made a wonderful jelly pie. "I got married and moved away and Grandmother died. I tried to make the pie like she did, but it never came out right. My daughter is a schoolteacher and went to a regional meeting this spring. She won the door prize—and it was your cookbook! I looked through it and there was a recipe for apple jelly pie! I made one right away and it tasted exactly like Grandmother's did! I had to write and thank you for making it possible for me to eat apple jelly pie once more." She signed her name and added a postscript: "I am ninety-three years old."

I applied for and received a small grant from the Mellon Foundation through the Appalachian Center at Berea College, and the money enabled me to travel and interview people whom I thought might have interesting things to talk about, including food. I accomplished my goal and interviewed around thirty different men and women. The interviews were transcribed by a treasured friend, the late Maxine Menefee. I had five notebooks of transcriptions.

It was difficult to decide how to present the material. I first read the transcripts as a whole and was impressed with the power of their words. I knew a simple approach was the best and decided to let them present their stories and recipes in their own words. I edited out my questions and wrote some connecting narrative to help the flow. I put their recipes at the end of each chapter. The index in the back of this book will make it easier for you to find specific recipes.

I wanted to stay true to their dialect (if they had one) but at the same time did not want to use misspelled words to convey it. I did keep the unique turn of phrase or rhythm in the arrangement of words. I wrote a short paragraph or two to introduce each person or group of people.

After all the transcripts were edited, I mailed a copy of his or her chapter to each person I had interviewed, and asked them to update, add, or delete. I got all the material back along with word that since the interviews Rossie Wagner of Bluff City, Tennessee, and Theodosia Barrett of Lebanon, Virginia, had died. Verna Mae Slone wrote that her beloved husband, Willie, had died the year before. Theodosia's sister, Mae Wells Ball, read her chapter and approved it for publication. Marje Owen read her mother's chapter (Rossie Wagner) and sent it back. Everyone cooperated extremely well in this aspect of the book.

In this book I have presented two women nearing their century mark who still cooked and remembered the old ways of doing things. There are women of my generation who rely a great deal on cream soups (mushroom, chicken, celery), whipping cream, and Cool Whip. And the younger generation of mountain cooks use as many convenience foods as cooks anywhere in the nation. I have found it interesting to trace the way food was and is cooked in the southern Appalachian mountains and the memories and traditions that have been carried into other states, towns, and cities, by younger generations.

TABLE TALK

Verna Mae Slone
Hindman, Kentucky

VERNA MAE SLONE *received a lot of attention in her late seventies when she wrote a manuscript about her father, "Kitteneye" Slone. The work was published, and the news media wrote about the book and about Verna Mae.*

I had come to the Appalachian Writers' Workshop held annually at the Hindman Settlement School in Knott County. Late one afternoon we sat in a hallway and talked. There was one high window that let in a slanting light. At one point the light touched her snow-white hair, braided into two plaits which hung down each side of her face. Her eyes are blue, and she has a soft mountain voice. Although Verna Mae is about two generations ahead of me, as she talked I was amazed to see how similar our backgrounds were; she grew up in Knott and I in Bell County, Kentucky.

I was born October 9, 1906, in eastern Kentucky at the mouth of Trace Fork on Caney in Knott County, so that labels me as a hillbilly right off. My mother died when I was born, and Father had to raise me and my six sisters. The oldest girl was just fourteen years old when I was born.

When I was three years old my sisters began to take me to school with them. They either had to take me or stay home with me. I remember they would take a quilt and spread it down in the back of the schoolroom where I played and slept. I don't suppose I learned

3

anything, however, I did complete the eighth grade by the time I was eleven years old. There was a law at that time that we couldn't go into high school at eleven, so I went through the eighth grade three times just waiting to get old enough to start high school. But when I was old enough to attend the Knott County High school in Caney, I just got to go there a year and a half.

I had to drop out once when my sister's family had a car wreck, and I had to quit school to go and help take care of them. Another time was when the Works Project Administration (WPA)—and all of those programs the government set up—came into being. Father and my stepmother were both too old to work on programs like that, so I had to take out a year or two to work in their place.

At twenty-three I still hadn't been able to finish high school. I worked for awhile at the Caney Creek Community Center, which later became known as Alice Lloyd College. There was a lady called Mrs. Wheeler who lived in Practice House. It was a building near the college, and ten or twelve girls lived there. She taught classes. We had to work and study. Then something happened, and Mrs. Wheeler no longer kept the school. I stayed on at what was first called Caney Creek Community Center, then Caney Junior College. It wasn't called Alice Lloyd until after Alice Lloyd, the founder, died.

Then I married Willie Slone in 1936. Even after I married, I started back in school twice because I wanted to write. I've always wanted to write stories and books and things. I wanted to put my thoughts on paper. I believed you had to have a college education before you would be accepted as a writer.

Because I believed that, I was the most surprised person of all that *What My Heart Wants to Tell*, did get recognized and was published. It was a book about my father. . . . When I first began the project I called it something like "In Remembrance of My Father," and I only intended to make twenty copies and photocopy and staple them together. At that time I couldn't type (later I taught myself to type), so I did it in longhand. Later one of my nieces typed the manuscript for me, and she took a chapter to her English class and let her teacher read it.

When Laurel Shackleford was doing oral histories for her book, *Our Appalachia,* I helped her. She saw my manuscript and wrote an article about me which appeared in the *Courier-Journal* newspaper along with a chapter of my work. From that piece in the paper, I received orders for twelve thousand copies just in the stapled form.

Later on someone asked if portions could be read over National Public Radio, and I said yes, if they got a mountain person to do it. They got Lee Howard, who is educated but never lost our mountain dialect, to read it. Someone at New Republic Books in Washington heard it on the radio and called and asked if they could publish it. I almost had a heart attack! They did, changing the title to *What My Heart Wants to Tell.* It was published in hardback, and later paperback. It got a lot of reviews. . . . I have been interviewed by television show people, have been on radio, and had autograph parties in quite a few places. All of this, and me thinking all the time you had to have a college degree before you could write!

Willie and I had five sons. The last child was born when the first ones were almost grown. I always say God sent me four as a family, and then, because I was doing a good job, He sent me an extra bonus in my old age. I was almost forty when the last one was born. The boys in the order they were born were named Milburn David, Orban Blondel, Losses Agnell, Willie Vernon, and Marcel Len.

I was always asked why I named one of my boys Losses. There's a little story goes with that name. One of my sisters had both boys and girls, but only the girls lived. Every one of the boys died. She lost so many boys she called them Losses. Just to please her, I named my boy Losses Agnell. Agnell was the name of my husband's best friend. My father couldn't pronounce his name and called him Agland. My mother-in-law wouldn't even try to say his name. We just called him Losses most of the time.

It seems we got the name right for him, though I hate to think it. He's lost everything he's had, the third time just last summer. He was building a new home and had a restaurant, and they both burned down. At times he resents his name, at other times he's proud, says no one else in the world has a name like him. Then he named one of his boys Jonathan Losses.

You know, I named each one of my boys Sarah Ellen before they were born because I wanted a girl so badly. Finally I decided the only way to get a Sarah Ellen was to create one, so I wrote a book and named the little girl in it Sarah Ellen.

After working on the WPA, Willie got a job with the Kentucky-West Virginia Gas Company. He drove a bulldozer and built all the roads and everything. He winched the pipes up these hills to the gas wells with the bulldozer. I was at home by myself a lot of the time. I loved to sew, cook, and garden, but I hated housework worse than anything in the world.

All of the boys had to help do housework and things like that. Willie Vernon's job was to get up real early and go feed his father's horse. At that time Willie had to ride a horse—that was after he'd quit driving the bulldozer—his job now was going from gas well to gas well and checking on certain things. The horse would be finished eating by the time Willie got up for breakfast. Orban got up when I did and helped cook breakfast. Milburn David got the two little ones ready for school. Each boy made his own bed and washed his dishes before school.

When the children were small and Willie worked hard every day, we always had a big breakfast. We had fried potatoes, fried ham, and red-eye gravy. But I guess what the family all liked best was chicken and dumplings—but not for breakfast!

We had opened Slone's Grocery Store by that time, which I operated; later we added a gas station. After the boys went to school I'd go out and build a coal fire in the store, if it was cold weather, then back into the house if there was some little chore I had to do while the store heated up. I usually hired someone to come in and do the laundry.

I loved working in the store and serving the gas. I think if I had my life to live over I'd do that again. You could meet so many people and learn so much about human nature. We got robbed two or three times, and we were inspected by a government agent one time. But a lot of funny things happened. One guy came in one time and used a curse word and said what in the *blank blank* did a feller have to do around here to get gas. I said he was to ask like a gentleman. I wouldn't let him have any gas, and he went outside chomping on his cigar. I always said I would not let a business run me; I'd run the business. And I always did.

Most of the guys in the region would put the gas in themselves then come into the store to pay me. But one time it was raining and a man came in, said he wanted a dollar's worth of gas. I said, "I don't want to get out in the rain." He said, "I don't either." I said, "If you want the gas worse than I do the dollar, you will!" He went out and got what he wanted. We became friends, and he always stopped there for gas when he was in the area.

Before electricity came in we had a spring that we kept milk in and other things we needed to keep cold. I want to tell you about something I did—I guess I invented it because I don't know of anyone else who did what I did. But I dug a hole big enough to hold a fifty-pound lard can. (We bought lard in fifty-pound cans back then.) I dug the hole back under the shade of a big tree. I'd fill that lard can half full of water out of the well each morning and set my milk and butter in that. Of course I put the lid on it. It really kept things a lot colder than you'd imagine. Then during the war years we got some black-market pipe and piped water from a coal bank down to our kitchen. Coal banks were places where a family had dug out coal from the side of a hill, just enough for their own use. Oftentimes water would come out of the bank. We concreted a coal bank up and piped the water down to our house. The water ran into the sink. We were the first family in Caney to have running water.

I always read anything I could get my hands on, even if it was last year's almanac. But I did have access to the library up at Alice Lloyd College. I'd usually go every two weeks. I had a cousin that worked in the office where gift books were processed. A lot of books were donated by friends. These books had to be screened before they were placed on the shelf. She would ask me to screen and evaluate the books. So I always had a lot to read. Before my last son was born I had to stay in bed for seven months because I'd had a heart attack. I averaged reading three books a day during that time. I read all kinds of books. But I don't like books that are full of sex and blood. I think books like that should be banned. I don't like for my granddaughters to read them.

My mother was an Owens. The Owens family were of Welsh descent. I have traced our family back to William Owens born in November 1750, married September 30, 1773, to Nancy, born March 15, 1754. He enlisted in the Revolutionary War in June 1776, under Captain John Cook and Colonel Brown. The Owens family had a tradition that goes so far back that no one knows just when it started nor why. They always celebrated the first snow each winter by making a large kettle of hominy. Back then we made it in a big iron kettle and cooked it outdoors—a bushel of corn at a time. Those of us cousins still living have sunk so low that we just pick up a can of hominy at the supermarket, but we still have hominy on the day of the first snow. We call each other to make sure we have all remembered.

Usually on Memorial Day—which we called Decoration Day for a long time—there would be family reunions. The custom started way back when we just had circuit-rider preachers, and they only come around once a year. They would preach the funeral for all the people who had been buried since the last Decoration Day. All the families would make flowers and pretty things to decorate the graves before Decoration Day. I've seen my folks kill as many as sixteen chickens and put them in a big old iron kettle to cook. They would make dumplings and take the whole kettle to the family reunion. They would also make up a lot of gingerbread to have ready.

Father made his own molasses. In every community there was always one man that owned a cane grinder and a mule, and he would go around and make up the molasses for all of the others who had cane; his pay was part of the molasses. My father owned a cane grinding mill. It had the motor with rollers through which you fed stalks of cane, and it ground and squeezed out the juice which was collected in buckets or cans. A long "tongue," or arm extended out from the mill to which a mule or horse was hitched to pull it around in a large circle. As the arm moved it turned the grinder. The juice was then taken to a big vat placed over a fire where it would cook into molasses. Boiling down a vat took the good part of a day; it took a skilled hand to make molasses. It also took experience to know just when the cane was ready to cut because if let go too long, it will dry out—cut too early, and the molasses will be sour and won't keep.

We would take a joint of cane and dip it into the foam of the cooking juice and eat it. It was very good. We also would get choice joints of cane, hold lengthwise, bite down on the cane, and suck out the juice; we called this juicing the cane.

Then there were the wild greens in the springtime. We loved to get out early in the spring and pick the wild greens, the plantain, shoestring—which some people call chicken sallet, others call it bird's-nest—and crowsfoot. Shoestring is a little flower that grows on top of rocks, and it blooms real early. You can eat the whole plant except the roots. It grows about five-inches tall and has real small leaves, and you eat the plant, flower, leaves, and all. You cut it up and use it just like you would lettuce. There are two kinds of crowsfoot. On one kind the bottom leaf is white, and on the other the bottom leaf is red. We were always told to get the kind with white on the bottom leaf and not to eat the red.

When Willie worked for the gas company, he was out in the fields a lot, and he always brought in a lot of mushrooms. They are not good if you don't use them right away. They taste the best [when prepared] immediately.

I make and drink sassafras tea; have done so for many years. One of my sons has the same job Willie had before he retired, and he brings me dry-land fish and sassafras roots. Some people don't like sassafras tea because they make it too strong. You want it so that you have to hunt for the flavor when you swallow it. It tastes like root beer. You can use stems and leaves, but the inside of the bark is the best. You don't have to destroy the tree. You can just dig off a few roots and cover back over, and it don't ruin the tree.

You take the roots and wash them real good and scrape off the outside of the bark of the root. If you just leave a few roots lying out in a room they keep a delicious smell forever. I like sassafras tea best when just brought from the woods. But, after the bark is scraped off, you can put the roots in the sun to dry. And a piece just two-inches long will make a quart or two. I sweeten the tea with sugar or molasses.

Then there's spicewood tea; that's what Willie likes. You break off the leaves of the spicewood tree and boil them. You can use birch the same way. I must not forget mountain tea with it's good wintergreen taste. We used to eat the little red berries on mountain tea. You use the leaves to make the tea. . . . I also used sweet anise. My son brings me sweet anise when he can find it. You dig up the roots and you chew them. It's just a small plant which has a licorice taste. . . . I love it. It also smells wonderful. I lay pieces of it in the house just to smell.

Some people gather and eat papaws, but I can't stand the smell of them. We also ate mayapples. Now they tell us mayapples are poison. We didn't know no better so they didn't hurt us! My guarding angel was taking care of me again.

You know, I believe in guarding angels. Oh, I don't believe it's really a certain angel or something in human form. I just believe it's God's protection. There's the devil also; he has his disciples. I don't believe that you can see them and meet them or shake hands with them. But there's the devils, call them whatever you want to, your inner self, your conscience, or the Lord and the devil, black and white, or dark and light, or good and bad. . . . There's two forces that are absolutely working, and you're on one side or the other. There is no neutral place. Do I make myself clear?

I am a member of the Ivy Point Old Regular Baptist Church, and I'm also a member of the First Baptist Church. I joined both. I attend both, and no one has asked me to leave! They call me a Very Irregular Old Regular Baptist. I go to services at the Methodist Church sometimes. You see I don't serve the church; I serve God.

RED-EYE GRAVY

If you don't know what red-eye gravy is, that's where you fry your ham and the little residue that's left in there, you pour a little water or a little milk in there and the brown bits bubble loose, and then you pour it over the ham. We call it red-eye gravy or bay sop. I guess we called it bay sop because sometimes the cook would throw in a bay leaf for flavor. Sometimes a little sage would be used.

CHICKEN AND DUMPLINGS

I don't like the way they make dumplings now where they roll the dough out
and cut it into shoestrings, and you have to use a knife to cut them. I made
my dumpling dough by the same recipe as for biscuits. I would pinch off a gob
of dough, roll it in my hands, and drop in the broth. Dumplings like this are
waxy and good on the outside but still so soft and puffy inside. I always took
the chicken from the broth but leave the giblets, wings, and smaller pieces.

DRY-LAND FISH

To prepare the mushrooms: wash carefully, split in half lengthwise, and soak
at least fifteen minutes in salt water. Roll in flour or meal, or, if you prefer,
dip in beaten egg first before dredging. Fry in bacon grease or butter. Some
people called the mushrooms hickory chickens instead of dry-land fish. The
scientific name is morels.

HOMINY

To make hominy you must use an iron or enamel pot. Fill the pot with water,
add one heaping spoonful of lye to each gallon of shelled regular white corn.
Pour in the corn and cook until the outer skin can be easily removed by
rubbing a few kernals between your fingers. Remove from heat and wash in
several waters rubbing with the hands until all the husks are removed and the
taste of lye is gone. Put into a clear pot of water, and cook until tender. You
will need a much larger pot, or more than one for the second cooking, because
the corn will swell. But it does not have to be an iron pot this time.
Homemade hominy is good just sprinkled with salt and eaten as a snack. It is
also good fried in lard [or butter] and served as a vegetable dish.

My father once cooked for a large logging crew who were cutting the timber from the hillsides here in Knott County. He learned to cook this dish at that time and taught us later, after he had to cook for us when Mother died. I used it a lot for my children, and they loved it; they called it "Gut Am Growlin'" because it smelled so good while it was cooking. My oldest son says he loves to remember coming home from school when it had been raining all day and finding a large kettle of this stew on the back of the stove and a big pone of corn bread beside it. That and milk made a meal in itself.

"GUT AM GROWLIN'" STEW

Potatoes
Onions
Carrots
Corn
Green beans
Salt and pepper to taste
Chunks of stew beef
1 head of cabbage, quartered
Sliced tomatoes

Peel potatoes, onions, carrots, and cut beans. Brown chunks of beef. Quarter a head of cabbage. Put vegetables and beef into a large kettle. Add pieces of cabbage to top, add salt and pepper, pour in water (preferably water in which meat has been cooked or preboiled) to cover, and cook awhile. Add sliced tomatoes and cook until everything is tender. Pour the stew broth over pieces of corn bread or biscuits.

CORN ROAST

Use young corn when the grains will still run "milk" when jabbed with a fingernail. Turn back the husk to expose the ear of corn but do not break loose from the ear. Inspect for worms, bugs, or rotten spots. Clean away all the silks. Turn the husk back over the ear of corn, and tie some of the husk ends together. Dip into water to wet the husks so they will not burn. Place on hot coals of fire. Turn once or twice while cooking. Let remain until tender. Serve with salt and butter. Eat from the cob.

SASSAFRAS TEA

Dig sassafras roots early in the spring—just after the leaves start to grow. Wash well and peel or scrape the outside layer of bark from the roots and discard. Cut the remaining inner layer of bark from the wood part of the roots. Cut into small pieces and boil in water. Sweeten to taste. A piece about one-inch wide and five-inches long will make a quart of tea. It can be dried and used again and again. It will taste bitter if too much is used in relation to the amount of water. Sweeten with sugar, molasses, or honey.

BIRCH TEA

Tap a birch tree in the spring. Combine the sap with an equal amount of water and heat to boiling. Sweeten with honey and serve hot.

SPICEWOOD TEA

Gather small limbs and twigs from spicewood bushes; break into small pieces and boil in spring water. Strain and sweeten with honey, maple syrup, or molasses. Serve hot.

MOUNTAIN TEA

Gather desired amount of mountain tea and tender stems. Crush them and pour hot water over them. Steep to taste, drain, sweeten if desired, and serve hot.

SWEET-MILK PIE

When we had leftover biscuits, we used them to make a sweet-milk pie. A sauce was made with sweet milk and sugar, thickened with a little flour, and boiled. It was then spread over split biscuits, alternating a layer of biscuits and a layer of the sauce.

Almost every family had its own recipe and way of making gingerbread. This one has been handed down in the Owens family for generations. They used to make it to sell at election time when the politicians would buy it to treat the voters. I can remember them making barrels full and placing them in the smokehouse where the spilled salt from curing the meat kept the dirt floor damp, and thus kept the gingerbread from drying out. The barrel would be covered with an old quilt.

GINGERBREAD

10 pounds plain flour
1 pint brown sugar
½ pound butter
½ pound lard
1 cup molasses
1 heaping tablespoon ginger (we used race ginger which came in the root)
1 level teaspoon cinnamon
½ teaspoon nutmeg
1 teaspoon soda
4 eggs
8 teaspoons baking powder
1 quart buttermilk

Sift flour into a very large pan. Make a large hole in the center of flour about a ⅓ deep. (Be sure to leave at least 1 inch of flour from the edge of the hole to the sides of the pan.) Put into this space all the dry ingredients. Mix well with small amount of the flour from bottom of hole. Add eggs, soft lard, butter, and molasses. Mix well with your hand or large spoon. Add the milk, a little at a time, mixing with the flour. If you tap the sides of the pan this will cause a little of the flour to fall into the mixture.

Keep mixing and adding flour from the sides and bottom until you have worked all the flour into a dough. Knead until very stiff, the stiffer and dryer the better tasting, and your gingerbread will keep fresh for a longer period. Pinch off a small piece and shape into a cake about 1-inch thick and 3-inches long. Place in greased pan and pat smooth. (If you wish you can roll out and cut into shapes, but our old folks did not. I love to see the fingerprints on my gingerbread.) Using a fork with a cloth tied on the end for a brush, dip into a cup of egg whites and smear the tops of each cake. This gives them a pretty, glossy look.

Put into a moderate oven [300-350 degrees] and bake until brown. Watch carefully for they will burn easily. Good served with butter, milk, coffee, tea, or alone, warm or cold, or several weeks old.

STIFFJACK CANDY

2 cups molasses
2 tablespoons vinegar
2 tablespoons butter
½ teaspoon soda

Cook molasses and vinegar slowly to the hard ball test or to 266 degrees on a candy thermometer. Cook over low heat, and stir carefully to prevent scorching. Remove from heat, and add butter and soda. Stir until foaming stops. Pour upon oiled surface and when sufficiently cool, pull until the candy becomes firm and of light color. Stretch in a slender rope, and cut into pieces with sharp shears. Wrap in waxed paper.

FRIED MOLASSES

1 teaspoon lard, shortening, or margarine
Pinch of soda
1 pint molasses

Melt shortening in an iron skillet. Pour molasses into skillet, add soda, and stir well. Cook until foamy or bubbly. Pour over buttered biscuits or pancakes.

Theodosia Barrett

Lebanon, Virginia

THEODOSIA BARRETT'S *black hair was liberally sprinkled with silver, but the black still dominated. She walked as though a steel rod ran up her spine, and she had a precise way of enunciating her words, though they were spoken with a Virginia accent. She and her sister, Mae Wells Ball, came to the Appalachian Writers' Workshop at Hindman, Kentucky, for a number of years. I was astounded when she told me her birth date. She looks twenty years younger than her age.*

My name is Theodosia Wells Barrett. I was born on April 26, 1902, in Russell County, Virginia, in the Clinch River Valley fringe of Appalachia. My father was twenty years old when I was born. He owned a team of horses and a wagon. He hauled loads of lumber from sawmills in the area to the railroad to be shipped to northern markets. My mother was not quite sixteen when I was born; we grew up together.

The place where I was born was very humble. It was a little two-room house built with brown cull lumber. It might have been a sawmill shanty, with a native sandstone chimney. There were a dozen big apple trees growing around the house. In front was my grandfather's gristmill and the road. A creek went by our place and turned the wheels that ground meal.

That creek became very special to me; it had many moods . . . we often played in the creek. We'd fall in and get our clothes wet, and Mama would strip them off and wash them. We had friends down the creek; in summertime instead of walking down the road we'd wade down the creek to their house. That was fun. I loved that creek.

My paternal grandmother had come from eastern Virginia to the mountains when she was a young girl. Her name was Mary Jane Israel Wells. Her father, William Israel, had been a slave overseer on the Hardin Reynolds estate and Reynolds's plantation at Cirtz—which was where the R. J. Reynolds enterprise first started right there in Patrick County, Virginia, east of the Blue Ridge. But the Civil War came along, and my great-grandfather didn't have a job after the war ended; slaves were free.

So he packed up his wagon and headed for southwest Virginia when grandmother was just a young girl. She told me about the trip. She and my grandfather traveled around and they kept moving westward, and they moved a number of times. Grandmother Wells was a beautiful woman, small with little hands. She was delicate. Her stepmother who lived with them did the dirty work. My mother said grandmother was just plain lazy.

Grandfather and Grandmother Wells moved away when I was seven years old. I missed them because I had stayed with them much of the time. When still just a toddler I could go over to their house, and one thing that was always plentiful on their table was honey. Grandfather had a lot full of beehives right beside the house. There was a little house in the lot where he kept his bee supplies. I used to help when I was still small, I would help to make beeswax and to fix sashes, and I learned to handle bees. I learned never to fight a bee.

Father had some bees also. One time he and Mother had to be away from home just about the time he expected one hive to swarm.

He told me to be careful and watch where they settled so he could get them when he came home. He already had a beegum prepared.

Sure enough they did swarm. I was wearing a little light dress that I'd outgrown, because I grew faster than Mother could sew for me, and I was barefoot. I walked in and got my smoker and fixed it up and went and took out the new beegum. The bees settled on a little bush that leaned over. I took granulated sugar and made a little syrup and put a little inside the new hive. I also put some up right close to the bush where they had settled. I had seen Father do it that way. Then I put the bees in the beegum and didn't get a sting. I was nine or ten years old.

When I was just a little girl my Aunt Bertha, my grandmother's only daughter, was about six or eight years older than I, and in the afternoon they would get the churn out and do a churning. After the butter was taken out Grandmother always filled a little mixing bowl with buttermilk and gave us the corn bread that was left over from dinner that day. We crumbled the bread into that bowl, and my sister Dora, Aunt Bertha, and I got around that bowl and ate that crumble-in.

My maternal grandfather lived three miles up the road on Wolf Pen Branch. Grandmother Horton was a big mountain woman. All of her family were sturdy and grew big. She had big feet and hands, and she was six and a half feet tall. She was born May 10, 1865, just about the time her father returned from General Lee's ragged army. He came home so lousy that he had to be de-loused and washed in the washtub before his wife would allow him into the house. He was my great-grandfather.

My great-grandfather was a landowner. His mother and he had come from Carroll County, Virginia, over on the Blue Ridge. He was very poor when they came, but he accumulated lots of land and lived in a log cabin. When his seven children married, he gave each one at least a hundred-acre tract of land. There was timber, coal—everything on it that the good Lord made it with. So my grandmother settled near the head of Wolf Pen Creek, and Grandpa built the first building, a big hewed log cabin with a big fireplace. My mother, the second child, was born in that cabin. I especially loved the big house and grandmother; she was my idol, I wanted to be just like her.

Grandma was intelligent; she encouraged me to read, and her cooking was the best I've ever tasted yet. She raised chickens and vegetables. She studied seed catalogs. Right after the Civil War they had a few little schools, mostly subscription schools, but she attended a school in a log schoolhouse that was called Shady Grove. She read everything she could get her hands on. She had *Harper's, Saturday Review, Review of Reviews,* and her sons were very intellectual; her oldest son went to college and became a teacher. He was a great inspiration to me, my Uncle Albert.

You could go to Grandmother's house on Sunday and by eleven o'clock, there might still be no preparation for dinner. But she'd walk out to the chicken lot, reach down and pick up a fryer, and take a butcher knife and cut its head off and, while it was bleeding, strip the skin and the feathers all off, and in a very few minutes she had it ready for the pot. Sometimes in winter she would cook on the fireplace.

After Grandfather died in 1925, Uncle Claude tore the old kitchen down and built a modern kitchen with a sink in it. But Grandma's cooking never tasted the same after that old kitchen was gone. Some of the other grandchildren agreed with me that something about that old kitchen gave flavor to Grandma's cooking.

Grandmother was not afraid to try out new recipes. She made cheese, and her devil's food cake was the best I've ever tasted and her cottage cheese and her butter. She had a big springhouse that was built right below the spring where water ran down through it. It was sulphur water but so cold that butter would be hard in summertime, and that's all the refrigeration she had.

I remember that my mother was a very good cook. I recall that one morning she had fried chicken for breakfast and made big brown biscuits. After the chicken was fried she made gravy. She split open one of those big biscuits, put gravy on the top, and gave one each to my younger sister and me. I don't remember the chicken, but I do remember that biscuit and how good the chicken gravy tasted.

My mother kept geese, and they laid eggs during the spring of the year. When it was goose-egg season we had potato salad, we had both boiled and baked custard, we had everything imaginable that could be done with goose eggs. Mother made another dish that I never ate anywhere except years later in a buffet breakfast at a restaurant in Salt Lake City. I found this, and my son-in-law called it egg soup; but I never heard Mama call it anything.

If someone came in at any time of the day, and she wanted to whip up something right quick, she took milk, heated it over hot water, dropped eggs into the milk, and let the mixture cook on low heat. She mixed salt, pepper, and butter into the mixture and it was delicious—very good for sick folks. It was sort of like poached eggs, except she used milk and butter instead of water.

Then there were Mama's fried pies made from dried apples. They were the best I have ever eaten and so was her buttermilk. Her corn bread was made differently from what we make it now. The meal came from my grandfather's mill, and my father always ground it. He wouldn't eat bread made from meal that he didn't set the rocks and grind the meal himself. Mama put everything in a pan, and she stirred it with her hands. After it was thoroughly mixed she took both hands and patted it out and shaped "hobbies" of bread, which she baked on cast-iron griddles. I don't know why she called the pone of bread "hobby." Some people in the mountains just say pone of bread. She had two griddles that she put in the step-stove oven.

In winter we always had a big dinner around twelve o'clock. When the weather was cold and the kitchen was frozen up, she would bake enough bread for us to take into the front room and warm in front of the grate, and we'd have crumble-in for supper and leave the dishes until the next morning.

My mother's brother and my father's brother decided they wanted to go away to school, and they enrolled in Old Dominion College in Honaker, Virginia. They roomed together. They went there for three years and transferred to Lynchburg College. After that they separated. Mother's brother, Albert, settled near home and started working as a bookkeeper at the mines. Father's brother settled in Wise County, but he and Uncle Albert remained friends as long as they lived.

It was Uncle Albert that encouraged me to go to school. I had gone as far as I could in the little one-room school. I didn't want to get married; I wanted to do something else. He stopped at our house one Sunday and said, "I hear you've stopped school. Now you are too smart not to go to school. You come on now, school starts Monday morning and you be at my house ready to go." So I lived with him and went to school. I finished the seventh grade. It was rather hard; we had some Latin words.

The next summer I went to Radford College, stayed six weeks, and got a teacher's certificate and started teaching in a one-room school with seven grades. The school was in the same county in which we lived, but I had to stay away from home. I got a second grade certificate and I came back and taught an eight-month school term. I went back to Radford the next summer. You were supposed to have two years of high school before you took that state review course. I got the textbooks they used in the high school and studied them before I went back. I stayed eleven weeks, and when I started to register for that second part of the summer I wanted to try for the first grade certificate. The dean said you cannot do it; no one has ever done it. I studied those books. I made good grades on everything but algebra. I had five weeks, and that gave me credit for two years of high school, and I got my first grade certificate. It increased my salary tremendously. I did do what I was determined to do, but it took hard work.

Then I went back. If you have a first grade certificate, you could enter college. And after I did that, I went back to Radford and had more than a year's college credit. I taught a few years and got married.

Then the depression came along. My husband and I were on a farm. He was older than I, and he'd been a timber man; we lived on a hillside farm. He'd loaned a brother-in-law some money and had to take the farm in payment.

I lost my job because I got married. Back then teachers couldn't work if they had husbands. There was a big frame house on the farm, and we started working together. He had sheep and a team of horses. I did gardening and canning. Our farm was near the Blue Grass area of Virginia. On bluegrass, the cattle didn't have to be fed much during the winter to put them on the market. But the Clinch River divides the mineral lands and the bluegrass, and we were on the north side, the Appalachian side.

We had a county agent who was looking for some demonstration farms and homes, and we were selected—there were four in a county—as a unit of demonstration for the TVA. We built up the place—kept a record of everything. The home demonstration agent from Virginia Polytechnic Institute came and worked with us and the county agent. We carried on with that but it was just too much hard work; we were working ourselves to death and not making much money. We did have a purebred jersey herd started, but the sale from milk was not enough for us to make a profit in that area, so we decided to look elsewhere.

We heard that on one of the big commercial farms they needed a manager, and the county agent recommended us for that job. We sold out and moved to the new job. By this time we had two children, our son Harry and daughter Barbara. Harry was nine and Barbara two when we moved to the big farm. My husband was manager, and I was hostess in the house and took care of the commissary. We were there for seven years, and my little Mary Sue was born while we were there—that was during the war.

After we left there we bought a country store on Route 19—at that time people coming from Florida to the north traveled that route. Our specialty was cured hams. We had customers from everywhere, it seemed. A gentleman who lived nearby did the hams, and he sold them through us. . . . While there my husband's health began to fail, and we decided to move someplace before he retired. We bought five acres near the Richlands school and built a house there.

While we still owned the store I had been taking some extension classes from the University of Virginia, and the superintendent of the Russell County Scotts High School asked me if I would teach again. He gave me a much better job than I had ever had, with about three times as much as I was getting when I stopped teaching in 1930. I taught for thirteen years.

My husband died and the children left, so when I retired, I pulled up stakes and went to Florida and lived down there for about twelve years. While there I got interested in the local history of my native county. I sold my property in Florida and came back to Lebanon, Virginia. I live near the library and the courthouse. I work full time doing research in history and genealogy. I help young people find their roots, and I've helped some of our families and other families that have been separated and lost track of each other. It's very rewarding. I am a happy person: I have no cares; I believe in doing things for myself. I have already made my funeral arrangements to the last detail—no one will have that to do—even to the number of pink rosebuds that are going to be put on my casket!

I have had three books published. The first one was *Pioneers on the Western Waters.* It was written about the people where I grew up, many of whom are my relatives and friends in that area. I just meant it mostly for the family. I had a thousand copies printed first, and they sold quickly, and then I had five hundred more, and again after that five hundred more printed.

You know there's always something to inspire one to write. A man up in Manassus, Virginia, made the remark to my sister that Russell County did nothing during the Civil War. I decided to find out. In the library and courthouse I found a lot of rich material which I wanted to tell to the world. The resulting book is not indexed but I gave my sources. This was my second book. The title was, *Russell County, a Confederate Breadbasket.* My third book was about a murder trial, entitled *Pioneer Murder,* [which] happened in 1817. By the way, the man who committed the murder and was hanged, was the grandfather of Devil Ance Hatfield, of the Hatfield-McCoy feud; this happened on the Clinch River.

You want me to talk about my cooking? Well I told you about my grandmother's and mother's cooking. I tried to copy my cooking methods more on the way Grandmother cooked. I liked to try new things. I grew every vegetable listed in the seed catalogs. I always had to cook a big breakfast for my husband who worked in the outdoors. He always said if he had a good breakfast he could go the rest of the day. We butchered a beef every winter and a couple of hogs. We raised chickens, turkeys, and that was our meat. Milk was plentiful; I made homemade cheese.

I learned how to do yeast breads—even won a blue ribbon at the county fair one time. Usually on Sunday morning I'd cook for company. I didn't know who was coming, but we didn't have a telephone at that time and if your relatives wanted to come, they just came in, and if other folks were passing they would stop also. My husband was widely known in the county.

One night my little son said to his father, "Dad, let's give our order for breakfast." That became a tradition. My husband would go out to the barn to feed while I cooked breakfast. We'd usually have sausage, bacon, or sometimes a slice of ham. I haven't tasted hams for years that were as good as those we cured. I canned sausage, pork chops, hamburger, everything. But for breakfast we would have some kind of fruit. We liked stewed apples or fried apples. Sometimes we'd have steak. He would hang a beef ham up in the smokehouse until spring, and he just carved that and let it cure. That made some of the most delicious steaks you've ever tasted. We'd have a slice of that for breakfast along with gravy and biscuits and some fresh stewed apples. We had our own York and Winesap apple trees.

Since I moved back from Florida I've had to change my way of cooking. It's hard, after having cooked for family and so many other people over the years to now cook for one person. I like a variety of foods and keep a well-stocked pantry, refrigerator, and freezer. I also have a garden and can beans and tomatoes. The surplus corn, peas, and spinach are frozen. I use less pork, less beef, and really very little chicken—very little meat nowadays. I like cabbage cooked with tomatoes or tomato sauce, just boiled in a little butter. I eat brown bread, no baked desserts; I haven't bought but one pound of sugar in years, and that's the little packets that I use to sweeten coffee or tea. I'm trying to keep my weight down, and I'm not supposed to use salt. I use vinegar on my vegetables instead of salt. I use herbal seasonings also for vegetables and salads.

In the morning I drink a glass of hot juice, either orange, apple, prune, or others. I also heat the skim milk for coffee and use generously. I am recently using Nutra Sweet in my coffee. The only dry cereal I use is spoon-size wheat and bran. In wintertime I have oatmeal. When I have grits I don't have bread.

GRITS

I use the recipe on the package, but after grits have cooked for 2 or 3 minutes, I drop in an egg with ½ pat of margarine or butter on the egg. Cover and cook over low heat. Makes one serving.

OATMEAL

Cook with ½ diced apple and ¼ cup raisins. Put butter or margarine on top and stir well.

BACON, EGG, AND KELLOGG'S ALL BRAN

Dice 2 slices bacon in tiny bits. Use a small cast-iron skillet. Sprinkle flour on bacon and brown in oven. Mash 1 small or ½ large banana, add 1 egg and about ½ cup Kellogg's All Bran or shredded wheat, crushed. Mix and pour over the browned bacon bits, first draining off excess fat. Bake at 350 degrees until brown. Makes one serving.

SPECIAL TOAST

Butter brown bread and place in baking pan. Put honey or molasses on top. Brown in 300 degree oven.

PORK CHOPS

Marinate chops in brown cider vinegar, minced onion, or garlic powder for ½ hour. Mix Italian seasoning with flour, and dredge chop until it is generously coated. Cook in oven until chops are brown. During first stage of cooking cover skillet, and for the last stage use broiler.

WILTED SALAD

Put small amount of cider vinegar and cooking oil in skillet and heat. Chop green onions and leaf lettuce and put into skillet. Stir salad until it begins to wilt. Delicious served with corn bread.

CABBAGE AND TOMATOES

Chop cabbage. Stir in fresh or canned tomatoes and 1 small diced onion. Season with herbs and vinegar. Add a lump of butter before serving.

CORN BREAD ADDITIONS

I often add leftover vegetables or meats to corn bread batter, stir well and bake. Applesauce is also delicious in corn bread.

BEDTIME DRINK

Steep a mint tea bag in ½ cup water, add ½ cup apple juice, and heat.

Bertie Holly Stumpf
Whispering Hills, Kentucky

I **FIRST MET** *Bertie Holly Stumpf on a dark December day when her daughter brought her to the Special Collections Department of Berea College Library, where I work. Bertie had bought a copy of* More Than Moonshine, *and wanted me to autograph it for her. Bertie grew up in and near Harlan, Kentucky.*

A couple of years later I heard from her again. I was finishing plans for this book and asked if I could interview her. She agreed, and we arranged a time for the following Sunday. "Come for dinner," she urged, "I'll fix some of the old-time dishes for you." She lives in a log house at Whispering Hills, Kentucky, just north of Lancaster which is not far from Berea, Kentucky.

Bertie came out onto the porch to greet me and introduced her husband, Howard. Their log house is very modern, nothing like the old log house I lived in as a child. In her eighties, Bertie had rose-blush cheeks, bright blue eyes, and beautiful hair which made a soft halo around her face.

My father's name was James Irvin Adams. I was born at Inman, Virginia, in Wise County, on February 19, 1906. I was named for Doctor Holly, who delivered me, and one of his daughters named Bertie. So I was Bertie Holly Adams.

We lived in Virginia for awhile, and when I was around five we moved to Kentucky and lived awhile in Balkan. I started school at five and a half in a one-room school. Later on a big schoolhouse was built.

I had eight brothers and three sisters. My mother was sick a lot so I had to learn how to cook at an early age. I missed a lot of school because I was needed at home. Finally I got plumb aggravated and quit in the fifth grade.

Neighbors had bean stringings, apple peelings, and things like that, and afterwards there would be music, dancing, and snacks. We went to those, and people came to ours. We had a good time. Mother and I would can beans, make pickle beans, shuck beans; we made kraut, canned corn, pickled beets, cucumber pickles, and different kinds of relishes, jellies, and jams. We also made hominy each year. We always had plenty of hogs to kill, and Mom made blood pudding.

She would catch the blood after the hog had been stuck in the throat. She would take the blood into the kitchen and beat it with an egg beater to keep the blood from clotting. My job was to go up on the hill and get pennyroyal to put in the pudding. She would put in a little meal and chop up and crush the pennyroyal, and that would give a little flavor. She also put in some salt. Then she put the blood in a big pan in the oven of our big Home Comfort stove. She would bake it for awhile then take it out and cut it into little squares. It was really good. It was just like a pudding with a reddish color. I also had to clean the hog guts and get all the fat to make lye soap.

You know life's a lot easier nowadays. Back home we always washed our clothes out by the creek. We would make a fire, heat a tub of water, and scrub the clothes on a washboard. I've seen Mother scrub clothes on the washboard until her hands were bleeding. I've done the same thing. When I was small I would get in the tub, barefooted, and jump up and down on the quilts to get the dirt and soapsuds out. And sometimes we'd hang out the clothes and they'd be frozen before we could get the clothespins on to hold them.

We never had plumbing, just a nice, big outhouse. Another thing, I never bought a pair of panties or slip until after I was married. Mother always made our dresses and underclothes out of flour sacks and feed sacks. She sewed just about everything we wore. When I got bigger, sometimes I'd see someone with a dress on that I liked, or see one in a store window, and I'd come home and try to draw a picture of what it looked like for Mother. She would cut paper out first and then cut the material, and every time the dress would look just like the one I'd seen. She was awfully clever with her hands.

Every morning of the world, Mother would holler at me to get up and start a fire. Sometimes after I built a fire in the cookstove I laid down behind it to wait for it to get warm. (Today I don't have to get up until I'm good and ready. It's good to be retired.) I had three brothers, and they would get in kindling and wood but never had to start fires. Somehow I was the one had to do it all the time.

In 1914, Grandma, Mother's mother, came to live with us awhile. At that time we lived on a small farm near a coal-mining camp where Father worked. This was a little community called Balkan, in Bell County, Kentucky. I was eight years old. Grandma's maiden name was Nan Gilley. She married a man named Haney after Grandpa died. He had been a schoolteacher, and one weekend when he was riding his horse home some men attacked him, beat him up, and killed him. It was a week or longer before he was found. Grandma never did marry again.

Grandma didn't have any teeth, and she was blind. She always wore long dresses and a big long apron gathered on a band which she tied around her waist with a big bow in back. She wore a little pouch under her apron in which she always carried a Barlow knife and a plug of apple tobacco. She loved to chew tobacco, and I enjoyed watching her take it out of her pouch and cutting off a chew.

She and I would always wash the dishes after each meal. Washing dishes seemed to be one of the jobs that she enjoyed doing. I can see her now, standing in the kitchen by the big coal stove, the dishpan of water on the stove, and the fire almost out, but warm enough to keep the water hot. I would dry the dishes and put them away.

Our Home Comfort range had a warming closet and a tank to keep water hot. Every night my job was to get a pan of warm water from the water tank and wash Grandma's feet. Sometimes I didn't mind at all to do this for her. But other times I didn't want to wash them. I would feel like hiding.

One day in the early winter of 1916, she decided she wanted to go over to one of our friends who lived about four miles away in the mining camp. This friend was very good to us. Any time we needed help or anyone in the family happened to be sick, she was always there to help. She was just like a nurse, always visiting and helping people.

Grandma rode on the horse behind my baby brother, Frank, while an older brother, Blaine, rode another horse. They had to go up a small hill, and Grandma fell off and broke her hip. She always said it was Frank's fault. Anyway, they got her to our friend's house and got a doctor and all. She had a long stay with our friend.

When people came to visit us Mom and I would pop a big pan of popcorn to have as a treat. We never had a lot of ice cream, cokes, candy, or cookies. At Christmas we would hang our stockings up, and Christmas morning there would be one orange, an apple, maybe a banana, nuts, and mixed candy.

In June when the June apples got ripe—Oh, that made me think of something! One year when I was nine, and June apples were ripe, I was in the kitchen, and I saw this half-gallon jar of moonshine sitting on the counter. I thought I would try it since I had never tasted moonshine before. I got drunk. That was on Saturday afternoon.

All day Sunday I laid on the edge of the porch, eating June apples and vomiting. I never took another drink until 1952, and then it was a very small one. Now I stay away from bourbon and moonshine. I'll drink a little wine every now and then.

When I was fourteen I got a job doing housework for Mr. Rouse, who owned part of the Creech Coal Company in Harlan County. He was separated from his wife, who lived in Pineville. He paid me $10 a week. This was in a community called Twila. The man taught me about some things. He said to me one time, "If you'll quit this job and go to school and then go on to college, I'll pay every penny of your way." The thought of going away from home scared me, and then about that time Father got killed.

My father worked as a coal miner for awhile, then he became a deputy sheriff for Bell County—Pineville is the county seat. Back in them days they used horses and mules in the mines to pull the cars out. Father took care of those horses and mules, keeping them shod and all, so he was a blacksmith, too.

When Father was killed he was doing his duty as a deputy sheriff. He went to Harlan County on a Sunday with a warrant for a man, but found out he couldn't arrest anyone in Harlan because he was deputy sheriff for Bell County. He saw two sheriffs up there and said, "I've got a warrant here which I'd like to give you," and he opened his coat to get it from his pocket. Now Father always loved whiskey and carried a little with him. This day he had half a pint and the sheriffs saw it. One of them said, "No, we won't take the warrant; we'll just take you."

"No, you won't take me, neither," Father said and they argued about it. Two of my brothers, Ken and George, were with Father, and George decided to go on down to the depot and wait for the train. Ken stayed with Father who finally left the two sheriffs, angry because they wouldn't do their jobs.

Ken and Father went to the depot and started to get on the train.

Shots rang out, and Father fell, shot in the back; he died there on the steps. Those men hid behind a little house near the depot and bush-whacked him. Ken just picked Father up and carried him onto the train. The train pulled into the station at Pineville, and Ken and George took his body to the undertakers.

Two of my younger brothers had hitched up the wagon and gone to the depot to meet Father, Ken, and George. While they were gone I was getting supper ready, and I packed their dinner buckets because they had to work at the mines that night. They came back in the wagon, and Ken came in and told me Father was dead, murdered.

They embalmed Father at Pineville and then brought him home and sat his casket in the living room. Neighbors came in and sat with the family all the rest of that day, all night, and up until he was buried at two o'clock the next day. The Holiness people came and took him up to the Holiness Church and were singing some songs. Then the Masons came in. Father was a Mason, and the Masons bury their own members. They took charge. They took him to the grave-yard away up on a hill from Teejay and said their rites. I can re-member walking up that hill and I was wearing a pretty white dress, which an older sister had made for me back in the summer.

Everyone of my brothers except one took after our father. They all drank, except one brother who now lives in Maryland; he never did drink or smoke.

None of my brothers ever went after those two sheriffs. My family generally was peaceful and had a live-and-let-live attitude. Other families had feuds and things like that, but we never did. So Father's death was never avenged. Father's wasn't the first death in the family, though, my oldest brother, Willie, had been killed two years earlier.

Willie went to Colorado, and while there, he killed a man and was sent to prison. He stayed in three years and then escaped. He came back to Kentucky. I can remember it as if it were yesterday. Me and my two younger brothers were down at the barn when we heard Mother start screaming, and keep on screaming. A man had come by earlier to look at a calf she wanted to sell. We thought he had done something to her and went a-running. But when we got up there she told us that Willie had come home, that he was in the blackberry patch above the house. He had escaped from prison and had hoboed on trains all the way from Colorado.

Willie said he'd heard that man talking to Mother about the calf, and he sat down there and ate blackberries. When the man left he had come and knocked on the door. When Mother opened the door Willie said, "Would you give a poor tramp a bite to eat?" Mother didn't understand him, and then he smiled. Then she knew who it was and got hysterical. Everybody tried to get her to stop. Willie said she'd cause the law to come and get him.

You know the law never did come to get him. He lived there in Teejay and worked awhile, then went to Lynch and got a job in 1918. He was a gambler; he liked to gamble and play cards. He was playing with two young men and they accused him of cheating. They went and told the Lynch police that Willie had cheated them. So two policemen came walking up the railroad track at the same time that Willie and George were walking down the railroad. Willie had a cigarette in his mouth, and they shot him right through the mouth. Didn't give him any warning at all—just shot him dead.

Those policemen were Halcomb and Coldiron. Nothing was ever done to punish them for what they had done. They were mean men and did what they wanted to do. They would harass people—be real mean to pregnant women especially. I remember what went on back then; it was not good times. Willie was brought home and buried in Teejay.

Now back then, there were teams playing ball. Baseball was big in those days around the different mining towns. And it came to pass

that the Lynch team was coming to play the Teejay team. Those
Lynch policemen were warned not to go to Teejay, because the
Adams boys would get them. The policemen scoffed, said they were
not afraid of the Adams boys.

My brothers were waiting at the depot. Ken said to one of the
men standing there with a gun, "Let me have your gun," and he took
it and hit one of the policemen in the back of the head and just about
killed him. Men in the crowd just picked him up and put him back on
the train. The other policeman kept real quiet.

Lynch had the U.S. Steel and Coal Company and a coke company; nearby Benham had International Harvester and coke ovens.
My first husband, John, was born at Evarts, another small coal town
in the same area. There were fights between the Union men and
company thugs; somebody was always getting killed, it seemed.
When John and I lived at Lynch and ran a boardinghouse there, I
guess there were about ten thousand people in the town. Now it's
down to about three thousand. A lot of buildings have been torn
down or sold, and there's not a whole lot there any more. When I
lived there I just worked and went to church. That was about all.

I don't go to church much any more; I have kind of slacked down
a little bit. Howard, my present husband, is a Catholic. There were
Baptist, Catholic, Methodist, and Church of God denominations in
Lynch. I belonged to the Church of God—a Holiness Church. There
were people in Lynch representing many nationalities—Italians,
Spaniards, Dutch, and Americans, both black and white. All came
there to work the coal mines.

But in spite of all the rough stuff, we had fun when I was growing
up. We had games—hopscotch, jumping rope, hide-and-seek, baseball, and jacks. We never played cards or saw a movie or had birthday
parties. We went to Sunday School and church. We were happy most
of the time.

When I was twelve my mother got religion, and that changed things a lot. We had attended a little Baptist church for years, but when she got religion it was at the Holiness Church. There were a lot of Holiness people around there, and they came up from Straight Creek and things like that. Father was hard on Mother when she got religion; he didn't want her to go to church. Then he got killed. Mother wouldn't let us go to any more bean stringings, or apple peelings, or birthday parties. She believed things like that were a sin. When I started going with the boys she never would let me go out unless one of my brothers was with us.

After Father was killed, Mother had to do something to pay for our groceries, so she opened a boardinghouse for the miners. I had to help her; it was hard work because we also served the men their meals.

When I first met John Griffith, he had been in World War I for seven years. When he got out he got a job at the Ford Coal Company. This company was located just a little ways from where we lived. I'd go over to the Ford Company's store and buy groceries.

One Sunday evening I was out on the porch and I said, "Mother, do you see that man standing down there? Well, he's my man even if I never get to meet him. I'll marry him if I can." I was eighteen years old.

I went out to milk the cow, and he come walking up the railroad, him and a fellow named Leonard Maggard. Leonard had tried to go with me, but I didn't like him as a boyfriend. They come on up and went in the house. Mother sat down with them and asked questions. She found out that John was married but separated from his wife. She didn't approve.

John kept coming up to the house, and we'd play the victrola and talk. That was in August, and from then to November he never even kissed me. In November he went to Knoxville, Tennessee, and told his wife he wanted a divorce. When he come back he showed me his divorce papers. He was going to work on the night shift, and before he left he kissed me. That was our first kiss. On Christmas Day we set our wedding date for February 15, 1924. We were married in February, and our first child was born in November. We had four boys and two girls; one little girl was born dead.

By the time John and I got married he was boarding at our house. I just kept on cooking for the boarders. I don't see how we ever done it. There were only two bedrooms, and we put four beds in each room. There were eight miners, and they slept in one room. See, four of them worked day shift and four the night shift, and they used the same beds.

John worked for the Ford Coal Company for several years, then when those mines worked out he went to work at another mine. In 1934 we moved to Lynch, Kentucky, and stayed until September 1950. From there we went to Washington, D.C., and stayed for awhile. By that time John was sick.

He had three heart attacks and something called Ménière's disease. He'd take these spells and fall down. He was afraid he'd fall in the mines and get killed. So we went to Washington, and he got a job with the Cook Grocery Company in Baltimore.

You see, one of my brother's had lived at Lynch until 1941 and then moved to Washington. We lived at his house until after Christmas. At Christmastime I went back to Kentucky and got our furniture. We moved into a house in Washington; it was called Fairaday Place. We lived there for awhile and then moved into another house. But we never got over wanting to go back to Lynch—to home.

The children were all grown by this time; it was just him and me. After that we started traveling and working on big farms. I'd be the cook and housekeeper, and he'd be the caretaker on the outside.

I never did change the way I cooked even when I cooked for

people away from the mountains. At the boardinghouse I cooked pork chops, chicken, potatoes, soup beans, cabbage, and things like that. The people I worked for in Cleveland liked my chicken and dumplings, corn bread, and biscuits the best in the world. I've cooked for lawyers, doctors, and all kinds of people. One lawyer that I worked for in Virginia said, "Bertie, I want you to make your apple pie and take it to the fair." But I never did. However, I did get lots of ribbons for the jellies that I made.

Did I tell you I got to go to Bermuda one time? For five years John and I worked for a Mr. Pittman in Maryland. But I was getting tired. See, Mr. Pittman divorced his first wife after they had four children, and married again, and had some more children. I was the cook. And I just got tired of it all.

I decided to visit one of our sons in Cleveland, Ohio. While there a Mr. Powell wanted me to work for him. They took me to Bermuda with them, paid my way on the airplane—that was my first airplane ride! They paid me $45 a week while I was in Bermuda, paid my way there and back. We stayed two weeks in Bermuda. I took care of their three children.

When I got back John said he was tired of Maryland and wanted me to go back to Maryland and help him pack. I know for a fact that John and I moved forty-five times, and every time we moved I was the one that did the packing. It was a sad day for me when my John died. He had a final heart attack in 1971.

I wanted to be sure and tell you about Howard, my second husband. Well, Howard Stumpf was born in Maryland. His wife was a diabetic and died about the time John did—as a matter of fact he died on a Friday morning and she died on Saturday morning. But I didn't know him then. We met two years later. It was in February, in Florida, that we met, and we got married on June 9, 1973.

While we were courting I said something about always wanting to go to Switzerland. Howard surprised me and took me to Switzerland on our honeymoon! We also went up the Rhine River to the Black Forest. We had a great time.

Howard and I get along good, are happy together—except for one thing. I don't know if I ought to say this . . . Howard is too crazy about me. Does that surprise you? Most women would be glad to have someone care for them that way. Anything I want to get he's happy and willing to go along with it.

John and I moved around to different states before he died. Howard and I lived in Arizona for five years. But always I have been homesick for Lynch, Kentucky. No matter where I've lived, Lynch always seemed like the place I wanted to be. . . . as soon as we could after our honeymoon, [Howard] took me back to Lynch again. Finally we moved to Versailles, Kentucky, and then, because I'd always wanted to live in a log house again, Howard had this one built for us.

I love living here; it's pretty countryside, there's space for a small garden, and plenty of flowers. Howard loves to fish, and there's a nice pond not too far away.

You know, it's surprising how many people you meet in the world and find out they are from the mountains! Recently we had a get-together in this neighborhood. I asked one woman where she and her husband were from, and she said he was from Harlan County. I asked him where in the county, and he said he'd lived in Balkan and Teejay! His last name was Owens.

"Lord have mercy!" I said, "I knew your daddy when he was a little bitty feller." I said I might have a picture to show him. I said, "My father is buried there and my brother is buried there." He said, "We'll go there this fall, we'll go. My grandfather's buried there." Now I'd been a-wanting to go there again.

Sidney, I've talked until I'm dry. I only wrote down three of my favorites; I expect you'll have more than you can print by the time you interview other people.

CANDIED SWEET POTATOES

Sweet potatoes
½ cup brown sugar
½ teaspoon salt
2½ tablespoons butter
¼ teaspoon nutmeg
½ cup orange juice

Mix sauce ingredients until dissolved, then pour over sweet potatoes which have been cooked and peeled. You may put marshmallows over top if you wish (I put 4 to 6 in medium dish). Makes about 4 servings.

POTATO SALAD

4 large potatoes, cooked day before and refrigerated
½ cup celery, chopped
1 small onion, chopped
Dill pickles or sweet relish
1 small green pepper (sweet)
2 teaspoons sugar
1 teaspoon salt
Dash of garlic powder
1 tablespoon margarine or butter
Mayonnaise
4 hard-boiled eggs, sliced
Paprika

Chop potatoes and mix with celery, onion, pickles, green pepper, sugar, salt, and garlic powder. Use as much mayonnaise as it takes to bind all together. Put into serving bowl, place slices of eggs on top and sprinkle with paprika. Serve cold.

SAUCE FOR MACARONI AND CHEESE

Milk, small amount
2 tablespoons cornstarch
2 eggs
1 teaspoon salt
2 tablespoons butter or margarine
1 cup grated Colby or longhorn cheese
¼ teaspoon black pepper
½ cup milk

Mix milk and cornstarch until smooth. Add eggs, salt, butter, and cheese, and cook until thick. Mix into macaroni which has been cooked and drained, and pour into 1 small and 1 medium buttered casserole dishes. Sprinkle pepper on top, and pour milk over that. Bake at 350 degrees until brown.

Lelia Duckworth
Morganton, North Carolina

MY FRIEND *Jackie Hull had told me about Lelia Duck-worth, affectionately called Granny Duck, and arranged an interview. We stopped in front of a tiny house. Granny came to the door. Short and slender, she moved with the grace of a much younger woman. Her hair was short and curly. She had on a faint dusting of blush and powder, and her fingernails had been polished pink.*

I was born on May 22, 1891, at the foot of Biltmore Mountain. We lived there until I was two years old. Then we moved to E. P. Moore's place up on Route 64. There were six children in all, but a sister died at nine months of age.

I had to walk two miles each way to school. We got plenty of exercise walking to school in the snow. The school was a long building with a big fireplace at each end. You'd freeze on one side and burn on the other. School started in November and ended the last day of March.

Mother always baked our bread. I remember the first light bread ever came into the store. We'd buy a loaf about every two weeks or when we could get to town. We'd take either biscuits or light bread in a bucket for lunch at school. We'd carry meat, jelly, and sometimes a baked sweet potato or just whatever we'd have to eat. Mother baked cakes and pumpkin pies.

I did pretty well with most subjects at school, but I was not good in arithmetic. Do you remember the *Harvey's Grammar?* Well, I guess that was before your day. I was not good in arithmetic, but I stood on the floor many a day and spelled every word in the blue-back speller. I stayed in school until I was seventeen. I got married at eighteen.

Father was a farmer, raised everything we ate except sugar, rice, coffee, and stuff like that. We grew peas, the kind you let dry in the field before you pick them. I've picked a bushel a day many a day and threshed them out. We always had to work hard when I was growing up.

A man named Lazarus owned a general store where we got our shoes and things Mother couldn't make. But she made most of our clothes. Mother did our laundry using homemade lye soap to scrub them clean. But we bought a kind of soap that smelled real good which we washed our hair with and our bodies.

We stored our potatoes, turnips, and things like that in the ground to keep over the winter months. Father dug out a hole, lined it with straw, put whatever root vegetable was to be stored in the hole, covered over with straw, and mounded up the dirt. Then he'd put planks vertically on the mounds of dirt. The water ran off the boards when it rained instead of soaking down into the dirt.

We had an ice house made the same way except bigger. We would cut big chunks of ice out of the river when it froze every winter. (You know, it does not get that cold any more!) Father would go in the winter and get enough ice to put in our ice hole and cover it up with straw. We'd have ice the next summer. The ice house kept the ice from melting for a long time. In fact, the ice would last from freeze to freeze. There were even steps going down into the hole so we could go down and get a chunk or take milk to set on top of the straw to keep cool.

Father always butchered a hog or two each year, and we raised chickens. We didn't have beef back then. For holidays, we had chicken because none of us liked turkey. Mother made pumpkin pies, cakes, and sweet-potato custards and things like that. We'd have coffee and milk, whatever we wanted to drink. There wasn't any such things as soft drinks back then.

Every Sunday morning Father would get up, shave, and dress while Mother cooked breakfast. Then he hitched up the horses, and we'd go to church in the wagon. On Saturday, Mother would prepare most of the food for our Sunday dinner. People didn't like to do a lot of cooking on Sunday.

Did you ever have to churn? I did. I hated to see Monday, Wednesday, and Friday. That's when a churning had to be done. If the milk is warm enough, you can churn in ten minutes. If it's not, you have to put a little boiling water in it to warm it, and then the butter will be thin. We'd take the handle of the dasher and twirl it around and around in the milk; we called this gathering the butter. It would bring all the thin flecks together into a thick mass. Mother's churn held about eight gallons of milk.

We'd hang up our stockings on Christmas Eve. We girls got baby dolls and carriages, cups and saucers. . . . The boys got things boys like. We also got oranges, apples, candy, and raisins in our stockings. We'd decorate our little green Christmas tree with red paper chains, popcorn chains, and things like that. My children had more toys and things, more decorations, than I did growing up.

I had Minnie, Edward, Ervin, Ruth, Ida, and twin girls. I tried to space them out. Ida, my baby daughter, shot herself on the first day of August in 1973. She had something called Addison's disease. There weren't but about three people in the United States had it at that time; it was a rare disease. The doctors told her she could never be cured, and I believe if they hadn't of told her that—. She got depressed. She was fifty-two years old.

I've seen a lot of hardships and sad times in my life, you know, but

I have had a lot of pleasures, too. My husband and I sang with two other men as a quartet that performed. I played the piano and sang alto. We sang together for a long time. I enjoyed it.

The Blackwood Brothers used to sing at the auditorium over in Asheville. We'd leave home about twelve o'clock, eat supper in Asheville, and go early in order to get good seats. We'd still be there at three or four o'clock in the morning! I always said I had to stay until they said "Amen." Oh I enjoyed those nights.

What do I cook these days? Well, the usual things I guess, beans and potatoes, a little meat, corn bread, and turnip greens. Sometimes I make banana puddings and cakes. But not too often. I've learned a few tricks over the years. Did you ever put a little pinch of baking powder in your egg whites? The meringue will have like little bubbles of water sticking up on top. They look pretty. When you make spaghetti sauce, to keep it from popping out on your stove this is what you do: Take a chunk of butter and rub it all around your frying pan or kettle, all the way around. Then you brown your ground beef, put in your tomato paste, water, and whatever else you're going to put in it. You put it on medium low heat and you can go to town or do whatever, and there won't be a speck of that sauce pop out on your stove.

Do you know how to take gas out of cooked dry beans? When they get good and done—when you've got your table set and everything ready—just lay a piece of light bread on top of the beans. Go ahead and pour your coffee or milk or whatever you have. Then get a ladle and take that piece of bread out and throw it away. You'll never have even one—any gas disturbance at all. (Jackie Hull, you quit that giggling!)

If you've cooked beef that was tough, well, if you'll put a tablespoonful of vinegar in your water the next time, the meat will cook up very tender.

When I was raising my children, I had a certain day of the week to do certain things. With seven children, I don't know how I got it all done. Every Monday morning if it wasn't raining I did the washing. Then on Tuesday, I'd iron every piece of clothing, iron the diapers and fold them up—I even ironed the socks. And I always put things in certain places. I have a closet shelf full of sheets right now, and I can go in there and shut my eyes and go along that row of sheets and pull out the certain sheet that I want. And if anybody moves anything, I can tell.

One time Mother got a cough, and she coughed awful bad. Old Dr. Anderson came to see her, and he talked with Father. "You are going to have to get Ivy some liquor," he said, "I'm afraid she's got tuberculosis. That will cure it." Father didn't question that it was consumption because it ran in Mother's side of the Dale family. Father asked, "How much should she drink?" Dr. Anderson said, "In every twenty-four hours I want her to drink a pint." Mother did that every day for about six months. Then she quit and never drank another drop. She lived to be eighty-seven years old! We had to depend on a lot of home remedies back them times. There's a good nurse I know. Her niece got sick with the flux. (You used to call it flux, but now it's called colitis.) Her bowels were running off, and the doctor said, "Well, I've done all that I can do. Go out to Granny Duck's; she'll tell you something that will cure it." Miss Ruby came out here, and she said, "Granny, what's good for the flux."

"You go to the liquor store and get you some good liquor," I said. "Put some of it in a cup, strike a match, and set the liquor on fire. Let it burn for about a minute or a little less, then put a tiny bit of salt on it, and the flame will go out. Then strike another match and light the liquor again, only this time let it burn until it goes out by itself. Give two drops of this burned liquor to your niece ever[y] hour. You won't have to give her more tha[n] six drops." The girl got better, grew up, and married. There's [a] lot of home remedies you can use if you know what they are.

I've only been in the hospital three times in my life. I was in the hospital with yellow jaundice one time, I was in for five weeks when I broke my hip when I was in my seventies, and the third time was when something got wrong with my legs. I had all my children at home. A doctor came and delivered them every one at home. I always figured it was appropriate to have a doctor at the end. A man started it, and a man had to finish it up.

Other remedies? Did you ever drink ginger tea for colds and flu? I raised one of my granddaughters, and we drank a cup of ginger tea every night, and we never had a cold or the flu. Some people put in a little moonshine, but I never had any to put in.

Do you know that Argo starch will prevent you from getting pregnant? One time a woman that was older than me told me how. Argo starch. The starch comes in little lumps, and you just take some of them lumps and chew them up and swallow them. I advised several young women to do this, and not a one of them got pregnant as long as they ate the starch about once a week.

I'll tell you a good cure for toothache. If you have a cavity, take a little piece of cotton and wet it with saliva, go to your spice rack, put some allspice on a paper and twirl that little piece of cotton in it, and push it down in the cavity. In less than ten minutes your tooth will be easy.

You've heard of people who have what they used to call carbuncles? Now, Leroy up here used to have a big carbuncle every spring of his life. Well, I went to the store and got some blackstrap molasses. I put the molasses in a cup, and put what sulphur that will lay on the point of a knife into the molasses and stirred real good. I made Leroy eat about a spoonful at one time. I did that for Leroy for two springs, and he's now sixty-two years old, and he ain't never had another boil.

A cup of molasses will last three or four weeks. The molasses and sulphur purified the blood.

You want to be careful with the sulphur because if you get too much and get wet, it'll make you stiff as a stick. Sulphur's dangerous if you don't know how to use it. Just use what will lay on the point of a knife.

When I get a sore throat I tie a nylon stocking around my neck. I don't get a clean one. I just take a stocking off and put it around my neck and tie the ends in a knot. Sometime in the night I keep twisting and turning over, and before morning I'll lose the stocking. But when I get up in the morning I don't have any sign of a sore throat!

You've heard about mumps falling on a man and making him sterile? Old Doctor Bob Pearson knew about home remedies. He told my father about a man they both knew. He had mumps to fall on him, and he just swelled up terrible, and he couldn't hardly walk. Dr. Bob said to the man, "I'll tell you what to do. Get about six cobs out of the hog pen, get some paper, and put the cobs in a tin or galvanized bucket. Set that paper afire and set them cobs afire." He said to the man's wife, "Get one of your skee-r-ts (that's the way he pronounced the word skirt), and have him hunker down over that bucket. Then you pin the skee-r-t around him. He'll be all right in the morning." The man was better the next morning and fathered several children after that. I told that remedy to every one of my children. I said, "I don't know if you will have children or not, but if you get mumps and they fall on you, you remember them cobs." Now they have to be cobs out of a hog pen. You'd have to let them dry out before they would burn. They's lots of good remedies, if you know how to use them.

At the end of the interview, I asked Granny if she would play the piano and sing for me before I left. Jackie urged her to play. She hesitated at first, but

then did play and sing two songs, "I Saw the Light" and "River of Life."
Jackie sang with her on the last one. Granny Duck got sick during the
winter after our interview and died during the following year.

BANANA PUDDING

3 eggs, put whites of 2 of them in separate bowl
1½ tablespoons flour
4 tablespoons sugar
1 cup milk
Several bananas, sliced
Vanilla wafers
½ cup sugar
Pinch of baking powder

Mix eggs, flour, sugar, and milk. Heat on medium heat, stirring all the time so
filling won't stick. When cooked, set aside to cool. Line the bottom of a glass
bowl or other container with vanilla wafers. Place a slice of banana on each
wafer. Spoon filling over the top. Do this in several layers. Beat reserved egg
whites until stiff peaks form, add sugar and baking powder; stir until mixed.
Put the meringue on top of the final layer of wafers. Brown the meringue, but
be careful, for it will burn before you know it.

VINEGAR TAFFY

2 cups brown sugar
Butter the size of an egg
1 cup vinegar

Boil all together until thick. Test by dropping from spoon in cold water. If it
crisps immediately it is done. Pour into buttered tins. Mark with back of knife
in little squares when half cold.

SOFT GINGER CAKE

1 cup sugar
½ cup shortening
1 cup molasses
2½ cups all-purpose flour
1¾ teaspoons soda
1 teaspoon ground ginger
1 teaspoon ground cinnamon
¼ teaspoon ground cloves
¼ teaspoon salt
1 cup boiling water
2 eggs, well beaten

Cream sugar and shortening until light and fluffy. Add molasses; blend well. Combine dry ingredients. Add to creamed mixture alternately with boiling water, beginning and ending with dry ingredients; beat well after each addition. Add eggs, blend well. Pour batter into a well-greased 13 x 9 x 2-inch pan. Bake at 350 degrees for 30 minutes or until cake tests done. Cool and cut into large squares. Yields about 12 servings.

MOLASSES PIE

5 eggs
3 tablespoons flour
1 cup sugar
1 stick soft butter or margarine
1 teaspoon ground allspice
1 teaspoon ground cloves
Pinch of salt
1½ cups unsulphured molasses
Pastry for 2 (9-inch) pies

Combine eggs, flour, sugar, butter, allspice, cloves, and salt in mixing bowl, and beat until well blended. Put molasses in saucepan; bring to a boil and pour over egg mixture. Stir well; then pour into prepared pie shells. Bake at 300 degrees for 30 to 40 minutes or until mixture is firm in center.

CUSTARD PIE

¼ cup butter or margarine, softened
⅔ cup sugar
2 eggs
3 tablespoons plain flour
¾ cup evaporated milk
¼ cup water
1 teaspoon vanilla extract
1 (9-inch) unbaked pie shell

Cream butter and gradually add sugar, beating well. Add eggs, one at a time, beating well after each addition. Add flour; mix thoroughly. Stir in milk, water, and vanilla. Pour custard mixture into pastry shell. Bake at 400 degrees for 20 minutes. Reduce heat to 300 degrees and bake an additional 15 minutes. Cool. Refrigerate until thoroughly chilled.

Fred and Beulah Hull

Morganton, North Carolina

FRED AND BEULAH HULL *live in the western North Carolina mountains in Morganton. I interviewed them one evening when the sun was just going down behind the mountain. I was a guest of their daughter, Jackie, whom I had known for more than a decade. She lived not too far from her parents and after dinner drove me to meet them. I tried to interest her in being interviewed along with her parents, but she would not agree. Fred suggested that Beulah talk first and explained, "I love to talk, and I might take up too much of the time."*

My name is Beulah Hull. I was born in January 1913. We lived out Highway 64 about three miles from Morganton. We've lived here [in Morganton] fifty-two years. . . . I was born in Cleveland County, in the little community of Caesar, here in North Carolina, and grew up there right at the foot of the mountains. My family raised cotton. There were nine of us children. I have no brothers, just sisters. We had to do both boys' and girls' chores around the place. We had to help Father getting wood for the fires and with the plowing and all that. We had it rough. We all worked together. We'd have probably twenty-five acres of cotton, twenty acres of corn, and probably two acres of garden. We all worked hard. We'd make around twenty-five to thirty bails of cotton in the fall. That took some effort picking all that cotton.

54

When I was nineteen I left home. I came up here and got a job at the knitting mill in Drexel and worked there for six months. The machines I worked on became obsolete and they brought us to Morganton, to the Full Fashion Hosiery Mill.

I met Fred at a corn shucking one night at his home. He was my school bus driver all the years we went to school together, and I never thought about dating him. I visited my uncle near where Fred lived. One night they had a corn shucking at [Fred's] home and I went, and he asked to take me home. He had a girlfriend and I thought I shouldn't let him. . . . But I did. . . . After that I couldn't get rid of him!

Me and my sister had an apartment up here in Morganton. After I went with Fred that night, we came back and I just stayed at the apartment and Fred stayed where he was a-boarding until six or seven months later. We got married in 1934, in Gafney, South Carolina. We waited until we could get started, then rented a house. We lived in a little white house for seven years before we bought it, then we came up here and built the bigger home. When my youngest child was ten years old, I started back working. I worked twenty-five years after that. I worked five years at a dry cleaners and five years at the hosiery mill. My job was to set type to print the boxes after the hose were put in, and I enjoyed it very much. They were a good company. After I left, the company started doing some other things, not exclusively hosiery. Then I went to Broughton Hospital, a mental institution, and worked as a seamstress for fifteen years.

We had three girls. I always kind of dreaded the teenage part. But the teenage years for our girls were the best days of our lives. They stayed at home a long time before they got married.

All three took after Fred and loved music. They've sung all their lives. The two older daughters can play the piano some, but Jackie went on to major in music.

When I was a child our mother did the cooking until I got about twelve years old. We cooked the things that we raised. We had beans, potatoes, corn—all of the vegetables. Our meats were pork, some beef, chicken, and fish because my daddy fished. . . . He caught all kinds, but catfish was the most common. We had plenty to eat and we never went cold. But we didn't have luxuries. We had to dry fruit in the summer. All kinds of fruit. We fixed up the turnips, pumpkins, and sweet potatoes for the winter. We canned a lot of the food.

To dry apples we'd peel, slice, and put them out on a riddle to dry. Father would drive stakes in the ground and put poles across on top of the stakes, making a frame for a platform several feet high. We called it a riddle. Then he would take a big piece of bark, stretch it out flat to cover the frame and thus make a platform. He'd fix it so he could pour the fruit on it and spread it out to dry. We dried peaches—just washed the peaches and cut them in little slices, maybe in five pieces and set them up facing the sun. We just left the hull on.

Mother sewed all of our clothes. She could just look in a catalogue and see a dress and then sit down and cut her out a pattern. We'd get salt in a hundred-pound sack at a time. She'd take that sack and bleach it out and use it for dish towels. We used flour sacks for pillow cases. Four sacks sewed together made a sheet.

I didn't get any further than the eighth grade in school. I first started in a one-room school that had grades one through seven. When I was in fifth grade a new school was built that contained grades from kindergarten through high school. I had just barely got out of the seventh and started in the eighth when Mother got sick and, since I was the oldest, I had to drop out of school to help her. I was fourteen. I never got to attend school again. When she was better, I went to work.

My cooking changed when I had my own family. I cooked different dishes and learned more recipes than my mother or grandmother ever did. You can go to the grocery store and get all the things now but back then you didn't. We had biscuits for breakfast and lunch every day, then corn bread for dinner. Sunday dinner was usually stewed beef, green beans, potatoes, and some kind of pie for dessert. . . . We had all kinds of seasonal fruit pies.

We had the family pies. The way Mother made what she called a family pie was perhaps unique to her. I've never seen anybody else bake one like she did. It took a good while for the middle to get done. But she knew just about how long it would take and how hot to have the stove. I still do the pie for large crowds. When it came time, she made a pie out of sweet potatoes. She poured milk over the sweet potato pie. And we would use whipped cream over the others. My mother never had any cookbooks.

We all have fond memories of our childhood, I'm sure. I remember Christmas each year when I was a child. We always had big meals. The big meal was always on Christmas Day. The night before Christmas, Santa Claus came, so to speak. We didn't get too much back then. Each of us girls got a little china doll. We thought that was the greatest thing in the world. We put out toboggans in place of hanging up our stockings. We got that full of fruit and nuts. We opened our presents on Christmas morning. We kept that custom with our girls; we opened our Christmas presents on Christmas morning.

We didn't know much about a Christmas tree back then. I don't believe anyone had one. Only after I was married and my children came along did we have a Christmas tree. Christmas tree ornaments that hang on our Christmas tree now are ones we bought the children each year to hang on the tree. They look for those every year. I am keeping up that custom by buying my grandchildren an ornament each year to go on their tree.

I love to get my house cleaned up for company. I usually have my family and friends home during Christmas. We do a lot of cooking of pies, cakes, cookies, and candies. Turkey and ham are the two main meat dishes we have.

Now Fred, he cooks. He doesn't cook as much as he used to, but he still cooks some. He would take care of some of the meals and then he would fix special things. . . . I used to love both housekeeping and cooking but I don't care about either now. Fred and I still cook three meals a day. The dishes are washed three times a day. I've done that ever since I've been married. Both of us got sick in 1971—I had a bleeding ulcer; he had polyps. The doctor said no more biscuits and corn bread so we use toast—the biggest part of our bread is toast. I have had to learn a new trend in cooking since then, and use less fat, sweets, breads, things like that.

I don't do much handiwork any more. I learned to crochet and knit years ago. I sewed so much for fifteen years and then made all my children's clothes back when they were little, that I don't much care for it anymore. I made my own clothes for a long time but don't do that anymore.

Fred and I do a little traveling. I have gone to the Holy Land three times and Fred has gone four times. I love to visit the sick and help someone out if I can. That's my hobby, so to speak. I love that more than anything else.

Jackie had been talking with her father in another room while Beulah and I sat in her spotless kitchen. Bursts of laughter and a line or two from songs sung by first one and then the other, came from the other room. Beulah shook her head and smiled indulgently. Their laughter and songs punctuated much of Beulah's narrative. Jackie came in to spend time with her mother, and I went into the living room to talk with Fred.

I was born in 1908 in Cleveland County, in a small place called Caesar. My Dad had an eighty-acre farm. He had some cattle and horses; he was known as a horse trader. He raised some cotton, corn, and wheat. He tried to supply the family with food. When all the work was done, he'd get out and trade horses. He'd buy one or two. And someone would come and buy a mule to plow.

The children were all boys and no girls. We just didn't know anything except hard work. We plowed the mules, hoed cotton, corn, and picked the cotton in the fall. Only one other brother and I completed high school. We didn't have much money to buy clothes, and the older boys just didn't want to go to school without decent clothes. But I went anyway and got my diploma.

We slept on straw ticks—for mattresses. Once or twice a year we filled them with fresh straw. After the wheat was thrashed in the fall, mother would fill up the bed ticks with straw, and then in the spring we would empty out the old and fill with straw we'd saved and stored in the loft. I slept on a corded bed.

We had good parents. We never got hungry. Dad tried to keep us close. He always raised a few acres of cotton for cash money and in the fall of the year would take us down to a big store in Austin and buy us several new pairs of overalls and some pants or a suit. He'd buy several sacks of flour, sugar, and coffee to last several months at a time.

He would kill several hogs, dress out the meat, and put it in a smokehouse. We had ham whenever we wanted it. We could sell some corn, if needed, for a little extra cash, but corn was mostly raised to feed livestock and to be ground into cornmeal. We raised wheat to make flour. We always had chickens to furnish us eggs for breakfast. Every now and then, Dad would pick up two or three old hens and take them to the store to sell or trade in on food or something. We always had one or two young cattle to kill for beef. We raised enough vegetables to do a lot of canning. Mother canned half-gallon jars of fruit, beans, and peas.

We lived just half a mile from a mill that ground corn and wheat. We had an old corn sheller (in fact I've got it up in the smokehouse right now), and we shelled corn which was taken to the mill. It was a water-operated mill. There was a dam up the creek that ran the water through the race; it would come down and pour over the big wheel and turn the millstones to grind the corn. That mill now stands in the fairground at Shelby in Cleveland County. It's still got the big wheel. It must be thirty or forty feet high.

Some of my other brothers helped Mother cook. She depended on them. When it was cotton picking time, Mother would take her big sack over her shoulder and pick cotton until about eleven o'clock in the morning, and then she'd go in to get lunch. We'd pick cotton until twelve. She would bake big pans of corn bread in the wood stove while she got lunch ready. She would wrap the bread up in clean towels—kept for the purpose—and put the bread back in the oven after the fire died and the stove cooled; the bread stayed warm. We ate corn bread, pinto beans, Irish potatoes, and fresh milk. . . . After lunch Mother would go back with us to the field. Mother baked a lot of corn bread. She had to feed several coon and fox dogs my brothers had, as well as feed our family.

We didn't have these big electric washers and dryers like we do today. We had a well. . . . Some black men came out there and dug that thing square and probably eight feet deep. They went to the field with a wagon and horses and hauled one hundred loads of rocks and lined that square well with rocks and made it round. The rocks made it cool and kept the sides from caving in. We had to buy a two-and-a-half-gallon wooden bucket—because the rocks would have beat a tin bucket to pieces.

Dad would say, "Boys, go take your bucket and get us some water. When you get there let the bucket down and get it into the north side of the well where it will be colder."

My family were not musical people except one brother and me. Dad was a horse trader and in some trade picked up an old pump

organ. . . . I was the one interested in music and singing and welcomed the organ. One of my brothers was a banjo picker; I learned to
play the Autoharp.

Leaders would come around for two or three weeks during the
summertime and hold singing schools in the country churches. I
attended those sessions and learned how to do shape note singing.
Later in my life when I got to be practically grown up, they had a
three month singing school in Shelby. Dad paid my way to go down
there. I can sing the shape notes pretty well, even a new song I've
never seen. Yes there is a difference between round notes and shape
notes. In shape note singing, each shape represents one of four
sounds: fa, so, la, me. You go through the verse and chorus singing
sounds and then you put words to those sounds. Do you understand?

We had a neighbor who did some horse trading. Dad traded one
horse for another horse to this neighbor up there, and there was some
difference between them. The man told Dad he would give him the
difference between the two. "I'll give you a hundred dollars between
them," the man said. There was an Autoharp a-laying there and Dad
said, "If you pitch in that Autoharp I'll trade with you." So he got the
hundred dollars and he gave me the Autoharp. I learned how to play
it. My oldest brother was a good banjo picker. I guess I had more joy
and happiness with that old Autoharp than anything else. I've got
two now, a twelve-bar and a fifteen-bar.

My brother and I played for dances. A lot of times we'd be asked
to play for dances. We never got more than a dollar or two. We
would play for square dances. Two of my brothers were good dancers.
We had neighbors who played the guitar and violin.

We'd meet at different homes on Saturday night and have a
"break-down" so to speak. I didn't play too many square dances. The
brother next to me was a good bass singer. I sang with him for about
eight years. We sang with some boys in Cleveland County, and after

we came here to Burke County we got with two men we knew, one was a good high tenor singer, the other was a good baritone singer, my brother Lee sang bass, and I was lead singer. And we called ourselves the Hull Quartet for a number of years.

The Hull Quartet sang gospel songs in churches. Then later, after I was married and moved down here, we had a neighbor girl who was a fine pianist and organist. She joined me and we sang together for a number of years. We sang in Virginia, Tennessee, and South and North Carolina. Then when my girls grew up they formed the Hull Trio and went out and performed awhile. They played at concerts; they won little trophies and things. I won some trophies playing the Autoharp at the Mountain Festival in Asheville.

My wife and I were doing some performing together by this time. I had my harp amplified and she sang with me. We always went to the Grandfather Mountain Highland Games. We've had a lot of good experiences up there. In 1971 at the 44th Annual Mountain Dance and Folk Festival, I got the special Masters Award in a national Autoharp contest.

Music has been my life. . . . The wife and I sing some duets and Jackie sings with us as a trio. We love our music.

BEULAH'S FAMILY PIE

Use a big oblong pan. Make pie dough and roll out in layers. Prepare whatever you plan to use: peaches, apples, sweet potatoes, berries, whatever. Put 1 layer of dough in pan and spread on filling, then another layer of dough with another layer of fruit. Continue until pan is almost full. Pour water over top until it rises in sides of pan. Sprinkle sugar over the top and dot with butter. Put in the oven and let pie bake. If desired, you may serve with whipped cream.

CHICKEN PIE

Use above directions for pie. Cook chicken and remove from bone, save broth. Prepare any vegetables you plan to use. Alternate layers of chicken, pie crust, vegetables, and a little chicken broth poured over each layer. The pie top should be dough. Then pour in chicken broth until it comes to the top. Dot dough with butter; put into oven and bake. It will take a long time for the pie to get done in the middle if you have several layers. Use your own judgment about how long to bake it. Bake in preheated oven at 350 degrees.

SWEET POTATO PIE

Slice sweet potatoes into thin slices. Roll out pie crust into layers. Put layer of dough and layer of sweet potatoes in pan, and pour a little bit of milk on each layer. Pour milk over the top layer when pan is as full as you desire. Sprinkle sugar on top layer and dot with butter.

Fred's tuna casserole is the best one I know. We've been making that for some years. I've got a recipe here for you.

FRED'S TUNA CASSEROLE

1 can tuna
1 can of celery or cream of chicken soup
1 medium onion, chopped
Pepper and salt to taste
1 can or package frozen garden peas
Milk
Crackers

Stir tuna and soup together. Add salt, pepper, chopped onion, and peas, and stir well. Put into casserole dish. Crush crackers and spread on top of casserole. Last of all, pour a little bit of milk over top of the crackers. Heat in 350 degree oven until bubbly and golden brown. Serve hot.

The following recipes were handed down to Beulah Hull. They are presented here in the exact words of the women who wrote them for her.

GRANDMA HUNT'S BAKED CABBAGE

1 small head cabbage, shredded
1 cup cream sauce
½ cup grated cheese

Boil and drain the cabbage when it is just tender but not mushy. Put in a casserole in layers—cabbage, sauce, cheese, until all are used. Put last layer of cheese on top. Bake in a 400 degree oven until mixture is bubbly, about 15 minutes.

AUNT LILLIE'S LEFTOVER POTATOES

2 cups cold mashed potatoes
Salt and pepper to taste
Butter or margarine to taste
2 egg yolks
Cloves
Paprika (optional)

Mold well-seasoned potatoes into small shapes to look like apples. Put cloves in for stems. Brush one side with egg yolks and a little water mixed. You may dust with paprika, if desired. Brown in hot oven and serve around meat.

GRANDMA HULL'S CUCUMBER SALAD

2 tender cucumbers
½ cup sour cream
2 tablespoons lemon juice
½ teaspoon salt
½ teaspoon sugar

Peel the cucumbers and slice them thin. Mix sour cream, lemon juice, salt, and sugar. Add mixture to cucumbers, stirring to coat each slice. Put in refrigerator for 4 hours before serving.

ESSIE BELLE'S PINEAPPLE FRITTERS

1 egg
1 cup milk
3 tablespoons sugar or honey
2½ teaspoons baking powder
1 cup crushed and drained pineapple
2 tablespoons butter or margarine, melted
2½ cups flour

Combine in order given. Mix well and drop batter, 1 tablespoon at a time, into deep, hot vegetable oil. When golden brown, drain on paper towels.

SAUCE FOR PINEAPPLE FRITTERS

1 cup light brown sugar
2 tablespoons flour
½ teaspoon lemon juice
1 cup water
1 cup pineapple juice
2 tablespoons butter or margarine

Mix well and cook until clear. Serve over top of fritters.

Haywood and Kathleen Farr
Swannanoa, North Carolina

HAYWOOD AND KATHLEEN FARR *have lived all their married life in Swannanoa, North Carolina. They own a two-bedroom white house with an acre of ground.*

Haywood Farr was born on April 22, 1906, in Traveler's Rest, South Carolina. His mother died when he was eighteen years old and still living at home. Jennie was the oldest girl and assumed care for the baby, Ruth, and three other small children. Haywood smiles fondly when he talks about Jennie.

Jennie was a very good cook. Anytime she fixed a meal you could say it was good; she was just that type. I remember how she used to make an apple pie in the spring of the year, and I never ate better poke sallet than the way she fixed it. She would make biscuits—she wouldn't roll 'em out, she'd just pinch off small wads of dough and roll them between her hands, and they were always the same size.

I never did any cooking. Part of my job was getting in wood at night—kindling, stove wood, and everything like that and then feeding the mules and cows. My brother, Norwood, was supposed to help me but sometimes he shirked his duties. We had to get up before daylight because we always had things to do before we went to school and after school was out we did evening chores and sometimes had to go work in the fields.

One time Norwood and I got to playing ball and fooling around, and we didn't get no kindling in. Father was kind of ill-natured when he got up every morning. So he got up the next morning, and it was cold and frosty. He went in to build the fire, and there was no kindling. First I knew, he jerked Norwood and me out of bed and whipped us. He made us go out (it was still dark) and get some kindling right then. We didn't goof off like that again.

Every morning Father would get up first, build the fire in the cookstove in the summertime, and, if it was winter, also a fire in the fireplace. Then he'd go to the barn. As I said, Father was ill-natured in the mornings. I don't know if it was habit or not or if something hurt him.

Mother and Jennie never paid any attention to him. Mother would just go on cooking when he grumbled about something, never say a word to him. Mother would put biscuits in the oven to bake, and he'd watch her. Sometimes he'd go pull the biscuits out and start eating them before they were done. Always, after he'd get his breakfast he'd be all right. He never would fuss at Mother; he'd grumble about something or other but not directly to her.

Mother was ill almost two years before she died. She wasn't real bedfast for very long. From what we know today, she probably died with cancer. . . . There were eleven children in all, five older and five younger; I was right in the middle. . . . Father hardly ever went to church; Mother would go sometimes. The family didn't go to church very often.

There was a big crowd of boys in the neighborhood who were close in age to Norwood and me. We'd gather in some pasture and play ball. Sometimes we'd go fishing. Usually on Saturday afternoons we'd all gather and go over to Keeler River which was about a mile from our house. We all looked forward to going there.

There was a big poplar stump there and we'd dive off it into the water, and we'd swim. That is what we did on Saturday afternoons in the summertime. Although it was forbidden to do anything on Sundays, sometimes we boys would slip off and go swimming again. We had a good time growing up.

The Ebenezer School would start in July, go about six weeks, then shut down because we had to gather our cotton crops. Then school would start up again about the middle of October; it would run to March. We lived about two miles from the school.

The first job I ever had was not full time; I worked on a thrashing machine for two seasons, when they were thrashing grain. Then when I was nineteen years old I joined the Marine Corps. Norwood and I were just walking down Main Street in Greenville and saw a picture of a Marine out front, in uniform, who was saying, "Join the Marines and see the world," so we just joined up. It was 1926. I was in for four years.

In 1930 I came home to South Carolina. Father wanted me to help him farm that year so I did. Then I worked in a filling station in Greenville until September 1932. My oldest brother, Mack, was . . . working at the Beacon Blanket Plant in Swannanoa. The main Beacon plant had been in New Bedford, Massachusetts. They decided to close it down and move to North Carolina. They started hiring more men. Mack got me a job. The Beacon Blanket Plant expanded during the depression, expanded while so many businesses were closing. The people in command of the company came down with the plant, but they hired local men and women to work the plant.

In 1933, a young woman named Kathleen Allen came to Swannanoa. She was the youngest sister of Mack's wife, Jeanette. Her family called her Kate. She and I got married in 1934.

My starting salary at Beacon was twenty cents an hour. They put me to working with the machinist, or fixer, on the napping machine.

When the cloth is woven it's still hard until the napping is pulled out. Napping is what makes your blankets warm. Then I got to be the fixer and after that I went into the rug department. . . . [And eventually] I was made overseer of the screen printer department. I worked there for ten years or more, then was transferred to the testing laboratory. I stayed there until I retired.

Kate and I planted a big garden that first year—and raised one every year after that. It would have been hard for us to survive without raising some of our own food. I had a lot to learn because, while at home, in the springtime we boys would plow the garden, but Father would fix lettuce and onion beds, and Mother planted other vegetables. . . . [Now] I raise apples, cherries, plums, blackberries, rhubarb, and asparagus in my garden.

I learned how to graft trees from *Organic Gardening*. You have to time it for the last of March or first of April when the sap comes up. You take a tree with red apples, maybe another with yellow, you make a sloping cut of a branch off each one and tape them together. If you have a tree, say the size of your wrist, you saw it off and then split it, drive a wedge in to hold it open, then you take the graft and slope it on each side and slide it down in there until the bark is even with the one of the original tree, and put two more—one on either side—if you want to. Then you put grafting wax on to cover it over. You will have a new tree, with the same roots supporting the whole thing! Whatever tree, say a red delicious, and you graft a yellow transparent, the limb will always be yellow transparent. I have had some luck grafting shrubbery, but have never been able to graft a dogwood tree. [You have to use] the same size of seed. An apple can be grafted on a pear tree, for example, but they have to to have the same size seed. You could put a peach and a plum together. I've got a horse apple growing in a pear tree. Last year it had a couple of apples. They were good.

Kate Farr is a petite woman and, though in her mid-seventies, she does not have much gray in her pretty shade of brown hair. An excellent seamstress, Kate has sewn most of her own clothes for many years. She is also a folk artist.

I was born on September 6, 1917, at Pensacola, North Carolina. I was the youngest of four children; Jeanette, Gary, and Rossie were all older than me. When I was nine months old my father died. Father was thirty-two years old; Mother was in her twenties, which was awful young to be a widow with four children. All she could do was go back for awhile to her parents, Grandpa and Grandma Gardener. Then she got dissatisfied with that and came back to Pensacola to the little house she still owned; I don't know how long she lived there before she married again.

She married a man who had five children of his own. He was the only father I ever knew. That made a family of nine children, but of course, not all of us were there at the same time; the older ones had got married and had families of their own. (Even in death we have never all come together. When Daddy Atkins died, Louise was in the hospital, and she was the only one that was missing. Every time we tried to get together one or more had to miss.)

In the wintertime on Sundays we would eat Mother's chicken and dumplings. Haywood always loved Mother's chicken and dumplings; he says no one made them like she did. In spring and summer, after we raised fryers, we would have fried chicken. She would serve rice, green beans, and sweet potatoes with the chicken. She made her own bread—biscuits and corn bread.

I went to one year of high school at Burnsville, which was twelve miles from Pensacola. That summer I got sick and had my appendix out in the Fletcher Hospital in Asheville. I stayed with Jeanette and Mack to recuperate and, that fall, attended Swannanoa High

School. It seemed natural to stay there and finish high school, which I did.

You know, Mack and Jeanette were more than brother-in-law and sister to me. They were like a second set of parents. I guess with her being the oldest and me the youngest made it seem like that. Jeanette and Mack were the best people you'll ever see in this world. They helped more people than anyone will ever know. Mack died in 1972 and Jeanette in 1979. Sometimes yet I cannot believe they are dead. I miss them every day. I try to go often to the cemetery to put flowers on their graves.

When I was seventeen I met Haywood and we got married. I worked for a little while at the Beacon plant then attended Blanton Business College at night. I studied there two years in subjects I felt like I really needed such as typing, office machines, and things like that. I got a job with the college, worked in their office two years, and then went to the Carolina Tuberculosis Hospital to work in the post office as assistant mail clerk; I did that about two years. It was interesting work but hard on me standing that long each day. Eventually I transferred to the switchboard at the hospital. That was the last job I had.

Yes, I garden some, but Haywood never liked for me to get in *his* garden. We had more disagreements about that garden than we did about anything else. My mother had taught us to get all the weeds out—to pick the weeds out from around the plants with our fingers. Haywood believed that chopping the weeds out as they did for cotton was fine. He suggested that if I would stay in the house he would do the gardening. I decided not even to step inside his garden; so he brings the produce to me.

As quick as one of us girls got big enough to cook, we started cooking. We each had our assigned tasks. Every Sunday night Mother sat down and assigned our work for the coming week. That way we rotated the chores. . . . We learned to do cleaning, cooking, laundry, canning, and so forth. When I was growing up there were some of all three families there. For example, Daddy Atkins's daughter Essie was the same age as sister Rossie. There would be eight or ten people sitting down to meals—and I don't know how in the world Mother could keep hot bread on the table for that many people.

As for other work, I never went to play in my life when Mother didn't call me to come and do the churning. We had our own butter that way, and also jams, jellies, and things like that. We raised our own pork, chicken, and occasionally, beef. We had the perfect place to keep milk and butter cold. There was a big old spring deep enough to put a water bucket in and dip it down under. Grandfather built a little trough to catch the runoff from the spring and ran it right down to the springhouse. That's where we kept crocks of milk and butter. The springhouse wasn't five steps from the house. We should have had it pumped into the house, I guess, it sure would have saved a lot of work.

Mother and Daddy Atkins had five children, one a boy. My main job was having to baby-sit. I was the baby when they got married; then as I got bigger, other babies started coming. Sometimes I would have to go to the fields and take care of the babies while Mother helped hoe corn.

Even though I knew how to cook some things, when I married Haywood I didn't know nearly as much as I needed to know. Haywood taught me a lot about cooking. He cooked some while in the Marines, then Lewis's wife, Mae, died and Haywood moved in to help Lewis. He did most of the cooking for that family. His corn bread is better than mine.

My philosophy of life? I don't believe we can ever make the earth a better place to live in until people change. I feel like we have got so far away from God that our young people don't know what it's like to have a Christian home. I think God had a purpose for each of us when he put us here. As we live our lives, we should try to do what he wants us to do. I have tried to think what God put me here for, and I truly believe it is to work with shut-ins. I enjoy old people; I've been a shut-in myself and know what it feels like.

It was twenty-eight years ago that I had a tumor on my spine which required back surgery. A friend who helped me so much with physical therapy said I needed to relax more and made all kinds of suggestions. One time she said, "Kate, why don't you come with me and take art lessons?" She talked to her teacher about it, said I was not talented, but I needed help in other ways. The teacher agreed to work with me. She was on the faculty of Warren Wilson College and taught art classes one night a week.

We started with pastels, still lifes—just real simple things—then she had us work on landscapes. My paintings have been exhibited and won prizes twice. Haywood has been a big help and encouragement to me. He frames my paintings and helps in that way.

Yes, Haywood and I have been married a long time. We never had any children, but Jack and Grover, Jeanette and Mack's sons, and their cousin, Kim, sister Louise's daughter, have been especially close to us both. Haywood and I have had a happy life together. We can't complain.

Grover and Jack always liked my meat loaf. Any time they knew they were going to be eating with us they'd ask ahead of time that I fix the meat loaf.

MEAT LOAF

1½ pounds ground beef
½ pound pork sausage
3 slices loaf bread, crumbled
¼ to ½ cup ketchup
1 egg, lightly beaten
Salt to taste
Small onion, chopped
½ teaspoon sage

Mix ground beef and sausage together. Crumble bread and pour in just enough water to soften the crumbs. Add bread crumbs, ketchup, egg, salt, onion, and sage to meat mixture. Put into loaf pan and bake at 350 degrees for 1 hour. If top is getting too hard, baste with a little tomato sauce.

BROCCOLI AND RICE CASSEROLE

1 cup regular rice
1 (10 oz.) package chopped, frozen broccoli
1 stick melted margarine
1 tablespoon dehydrated onion, or ½ cup chopped onion
1 can cream of chicken soup
Grated cheese

Prepare rice and broccoli according to directions, except undercook broccoli. Drain. Combine with all other ingredients except cheese. Melt butter in dish and add all together. Top with cheese. Bake at 350 degrees for 20 minutes or until bubbly.

This is called a friendship cake because you have to look for friends to divide the starter with or it will overflow your containers!

FRIENDSHIP CAKE

SOURDOUGH STARTER AND FEEDER

1 cup flour
½ cup sugar
1 cup milk

Mix well and keep starter in refrigerator and stir daily. Feed 1 cup flour, 1 cup sugar, and 1 cup milk on first and fifth days. Bake on tenth day. When you bake, keep 1 cup starter, and give one cup to a friend.

CAKE

2 cups flour
2 cups starter
1 cup sugar
2 eggs
1 teaspoon vanilla
⅔ cup oil
½ teaspoon cinnamon
½ teaspoon soda
2 teaspoons baking powder
1 teaspoon salt

Mix the above ingredients and pour into a greased and floured 9 x 13-inch pan, or 2 round or square pans.

TOPPING

½ cup melted margarine
1 tablespoon flour
1 tablespoon cinnamon
1 cup brown sugar

Mix and pour topping over cake batter; swirl in, but not deep. Bake 35 to 40 minutes at 350 degrees.

This note was attached to the following recipe for brandied fruit when I first got a copy years ago: "This recipe came from the original start of the brandied fruit and is way over a hundred years old. It is a magic potion that must be handled with respect. The one with whom you share this recipe must be worthy. When you have three cups of fruit you may share 1½ cups with a friend. Always keep 1½ cups starter in a jar for yourself."

BRANDIED FRUIT

1 cup sugar
1 cup fruit: peaches, pineapple chunks, and cherries

Mix sugar into fruit mixture, put in a clean jar (an apothecary jar is best because the cover is not tight) and let set in a warm place for 2 weeks. Keep in a warm place close to oven or range top. Never refrigerate. Every 2 weeks add 1 cup drained fruit and 1 cup sugar—never add more often than 2 weeks. Use a wooden spoon to stir mixture to dissolve sugar. When you divide, do so before adding fruit and sugar. If you delay a day or so before adding fruit, then add 2 weeks from that day. Good over ice cream, sherbet, cake, meats, and so forth.

Ruth Farr Porcher
Swannanoa, North Carolina

RUTH FARR PORCHER *was born on a cotton farm May 7, 1918, at Travelers Rest, South Carolina. She was the baby sister in Haywood Farr's family. A small, dark-haired woman, she has one of the softest smiles I've ever seen. She is an excellent cook and a good seamstress. After I had interviewed Haywood and Kate, Ruth came across the Swannanoa River to their house, and I interviewed her at the kitchen table.*

My name is Ruth Farr Porcher. My father's name was William Riley Mack Farr, but he was called Mack. My mother was Lula Artens Hodgens. She grew up in Travelers Rest. In earlier days both of my grandfathers had lived on big plantations, but after the Civil War they lost their money. We lived closer to Greenville, South Carolina, at that time. My mother's people had a big farm. My grandmother's name was Eudora, my grandfather, Will Hodgens. Grandpa Hodgens had a big farm; he had more than we had. Well, I guess we would have had more if Father had not been drinking. He practically went through everything we had by drinking.

My mother was only forty-eight years old when she died. I don't know what killed her—probably overwork and having so many children. Our sister, Jennie, raised us little children. She always seemed to know when one of us was not sleeping well, and she'd be right there saying, "What's the matter?" She was a good mother. There were just four of us by then: Ruby, Blease, Bill, and me. I was the baby in the family. The older ones had married and moved away. There were eleven of us in all: Lewis was the oldest, and then there was one that died between Lewis and Jennie. Mack was after Jennie, then came Beulah.

We lived in a big two-story farmhouse. Travelers Rest is in kind of flat country. Nobody lived close by us, although you could see houses in the distance. We never went hungry or cold in the winter; Father provided for us. Father had a peach orchard, and there were pear and apple trees, grape vines, and a raspberry patch. We raised watermelons and cantaloupes.

I had to help on the farm just as soon as I got big enough. I was the "water boy." I had to carry water, and I wouldn't more than get to the house until Father would holler for more water, and I'd have to go back. Jennie would help me draw fresh water out of the well. I did that until I got big enough to hoe cotton. In late summer we had school for six weeks; then school would be out for six weeks when we had to pick cotton. Then school would start again. When the sun was out you really had to work cotton because when it got rained on it lowered the price.

We had to work hard on the farm but we had a lot of fun, and there were plenty of good things to eat in the summertime. Jennie stayed in the house and did the cooking and the cleaning. We worked the farm, and I guess that's why I don't like to cook today, because I never was brought up to it. I just don't take the interest in it that I should.

Jennie was engaged to be married when my mother died. She asked Lynn to marry somebody else because she wasn't going to leave us. She stayed and kept house for us for twelve years—until I was sixteen years old. Then she married Lynn after all. He'd waited all that time for her. He was a good husband to her. They had two boys.

Blease and Ruby are the only two in the family that finished high school. Bill went through seventh grade. I was in the ninth grade in the springtime; the bus had a wreck (a car hit the back end of the bus where I was sitting) and it broke my collarbone. The doctor wouldn't let me go back to school because I had a real deep cold. It was rainy weather, and he thought I might get pneumonia, so I didn't go back. Then when I was going to go into the tenth grade that fall, I didn't want to go, so I talked Father into letting me quit.

But at home there was just the same old stuff to do: work on the farm, or cleaning the yard, or helping Jennie with the housework. We had a big yard and no grass, so back then we would cut down dogwood sprouts, take the leaves off, and tie two or three of them together. We called that a brush broom. We'd have to sweep the smooth yellow dirt of the yard with a brush broom every week.

Wash days were real hard work. We had a big black wash pot. We had to go to one of the tenant houses and carry water from a well there for the pot, because the water in our well was very hard. The other well had soft water. Father would go down and build a fire under the black pot. Then he would draw up water from our well and fill three big tubs. We had to rub the clothes on a washboard real hard to get all the dirt out. We used cakes of homemade lye soap for this. After the clothes were washed in the soft water, they would be put into hard water in another tub to be rinsed, then on into the third for a final rinse. Then Jennie put all the white clothes into the black pot of soft water and boiled them until they were snow white. Finally the white clothes were put in a pan where bluing had been added to the water. Then everything was hung on lines with clothespins holding them in place.

Jennie always had beautiful flowers alongside the road that went by our house. She would plant four-o'clocks, and in the afternoons you could smell them all over the place. She had our long porch covered with flowers. She made her own pots with hammer and nails and wood. She made all the chicken coops. She stayed busy. But she was always good to us children.

We attended the Baptist church. Going to church was about the only social life we had. We weren't allowed any games on Sunday. We went to church in the morning then sat on the porch and stayed very quiet in the afternoon and then back to church Sunday night. Quite often friends of the family would come home with us after church Sunday morning for dinner. On Saturdays Jennie would bake cakes and pies and bake chicken. Through the week we would do our usual things until Wednesday night, then we'd go to prayer meeting.

Jennie was one of the best cooks you ever saw. She never went by a recipe as far as I know. I remember one time some of us went to visit Jennie unexpectedly. We got there early, and I asked what I could do to help with dinner. She said she didn't have a recipe in the house unless it was on a can.

She would bake devil's food cakes with buttermilk and soda; she'd make thin layers and put white icing between them. She'd make it on Friday and let it sit until Sunday. By that time it would be real moist.

Sometimes she'd make a pound cake on Monday morning. She'd use a pound of butter, a pound of sugar, and twelve eggs [which make a pound]. After the cake was baked, she'd put it in one of those big old cheese bins and keep it there until Saturday or Sunday; when she cut it, it was delicious.

Jennie fixed so many good things to eat, it would be hard to pick a favorite. Just the other day Kate and I were talking about Jennie's sweet-potato cobbler. She'd peel the potatoes, slice them long ways, and put them on to boil until they were a little tender; then she'd put them in sugar and lots of butter. She made dough for the crust, put it in the oven, and cooked it really slow. I reckon she did it in layers: potatoes, butter, then sugar. She'd roll out a hunk of dough larger than for a biscuit, and she'd stretch it out thin and place over the top.

After that was done she'd pour in a little of the water from boiling the potatoes. Then she'd bake the cobbler.

Jennie made the best egg custard and chocolate custard ever was. She would take a knife and slide it down between the custard and the pan and slide it out on the plate; it never tore, and it was never tough. In wintertime she would make stack pies out of pumpkin. She'd stack them one on top of the other. They were delicious.

Jennie ordered material for some clothes out of the Sears-Roebuck catalogue. She used to make slips and underclothes out of flour sacks. At night she would sit doing tatting which she would sew on our slips to make them pretty. Usually in the springtime they would take us to town and buy us a pair of black patent-leather shoes and socks. In the fall we would get a pair of high-top shoes which had to do us for six more months.

I don't remember ever having a Christmas tree; I don't think anyone did at that time. But as I grew up, Jennie would make a big fruitcake right after Thanksgiving. She used black walnuts, raisins, and stuff like that. We had a big old table in the dining room at which about twelve people could sit. Jennie just kept that table loaded with food. There'd be chicken and dumplings . . . and other good things to eat at Thanksgiving, Christmas, and just about any other day of the year.

All the Farr men seem to like sweets. In the morning Father always had molasses and there was honey. Jennie made preserves and jelly which were served all the time. She made biscuits every morning. In the summertime we had ice-cold milk to drink because we had an icebox. But is wasn't big enough to keep all our food in. Jennie came up with the solution.

Jennie dug a hole about three feet deep under a pear tree behind the smokehouse where it was shady. She lined the bottom of the hole with planks and made a wire screen to cover the top. She churned every day and put butter into molds. Then the butter would be put into buckets, and we'd lower them into the hole. Everything kept nice and cold in the hole.

Jennie used this same idea for flowers in the wintertime. She dug the hole and somehow contrived to have a shelf of solid dirt running around the sides. She put logs around the top of the hole like a little house. She'd put her flowers all around on that step. She made a door out of boards. She would cover it at night when it was cold. On pretty days she'd uncover the hole so the sun could shine in. It was a little bit like a greenhouse, I guess. Her flowers would keep all winter.

We all had some good times together. Oh, we'd have our little arguments and stuff until Father would step in on it. We had a lot of fun. They opened up a Civilian Conservation Corps for boys and men. Blease went into the 3-C (that's what it was called) after he finished high school. Jennie had her own buggy and mule, and she'd take us places. When Blease went to the 3-C Camp, he got a small check ever so often, almost all of which he saved and bought a car. He left it at home, telling Bill he could use it any time Jennie didn't need it, but it had to be there Sunday morning and night for us to go to church. Bill was real good about it and used Blease's car until he got married and got a car of his own.

My brother Mack married a woman named Jeanette and they took in boarders here in Swannanoa. When Jennie got married and moved to Easley, South Carolina, Lewis and his wife moved into the house with Father. I didn't like my sister-in-law, she was different from us and liked to stir up trouble between people. One evening I had a date with this boy, and we sat in the living room and talked, just as we usually did when we had dates. There was no place to go except to church. Father had never said a word against my dating boys.

The next morning Mae said, "You'd better go right back to your room and wait because your daddy's real mad at you." I asked whatever for, and she said, "Well, he stood right there at the door and listened to every word you said to that boy last night." I said why didn't he come on in; we never said a thing that he would not have wanted to hear. But that scared me because Father had an awful temper. I decided to just stay there in the kitchen until he came down. When Father came in he never said a word. I just didn't care for Mae at all.

Mae had a little girl, Kelly, who was about two years old, and she just wanted me to tend to her all the time and do all the housework. I was never really satisfied after Jennie left home. Then word came that Jennie was expecting her first baby. She was not doing too well; she had these real bad nosebleeds. Father sent me to stay with her until the baby came. Then Jeanette and Mack wanted me to come up to Swannanoa and help Jeanette with boarders, and take care of little Jack who had just been born. But I was never really satisfied staying with them either. I don't know, it seemed like my whole life was just mixed-up.

One day I was learning to skate out on the street and I met R. L. Pretty soon we started going together. R. L. and I got married and moved in the house with his mother. I found out he was just a regular mama's boy, and she bossed everybody and everything. She wouldn't let him move out, although his daddy tried to find us a house to live in. We didn't move out until Don, our second child, was born. Then the war started and R. L. went to Newport News, Virginia, to the shipyard, and he took me and the two children back to my father's house. I waited until he got us a place in Newport News. We lived there for about twenty-three months. I loved it.

I didn't know how to cook until we lived on our own in Newport News. We lived in a duplex, and Mrs. Brown lived in the other side of the house, and there was just a wall between our kitchens. Her husband and R. L. both worked second shift. She suggested that we cook the same things for dinner, and she'd show me how step by step. She taught me how to read and follow recipes. She was like a mother to me. She also insisted that I do the dishes and clean up the kitchen just as soon as we finished a meal. She said that was a good habit to get into.

We got along real good; R. L. had a good job. Then when World War II was shaping up to end, his mother started writing him. The pressure was so great, and he had never in his life not done what his mother wanted, so we moved back in with her. Eventually we bought a place out there behind the Swannanoa Schoolhouse, on Bee Tree Road. Later we built a house in Grovemont and lived there. My daughter, Carol, was born there. All this time, his mother kept telling him what to do. He'd run to do her bidding every time. I was real unhappy. Finally R. L. and I got a divorce; I couldn't take it any more. I've just had a mixed-up life, really and truly I have, but the past twelve years have been the happiest.

I met Joe Porcher and we got married. Joe has been so good to me; he's made life wonderful. We still live here in Swannanoa, right there across the bridge. My children all live around here which makes it good for me. Jerry lives up past Camp Rockmont, Carol lives in Grovemont, and Don lives in Beverly Hills next to Asheville.

Favorite foods? I guess I'd have to say pound cake is the favorite at our house because that's what Joe always wants to eat. Anything sweet is my favorite! I have always liked to bake cakes. I have a real simple recipe which uses self-rising flour. It makes two big layers. You can put any kind of icing on it. Around Christmastime everyone wants me to make coconut cake. My children wouldn't know what to do if they didn't have fresh coconut cake. I always fix one.

SARAH BEYA'S MEAT LOAF

1 pound ground chuck
½ to ¾ cup crumbled saltines
¼ cup milk or canned cream
1 egg
1 tablespoon minced onion
Salt, pepper, dash of garlic
1 tablespoon Worcestershire sauce (double or triple if needed)

Butter frying pan. Roll out meat loaf and brown on both sides. Take out and put in casserole.

SAUCE

¼ cup ketchup
Sprinkle of oregano
1 small onion, chopped
1 teaspoon mustard
3 or 4 tablespoons brown sugar

Mix ingredients well. Pour sauce on top. Bake 1 hour at 300 degrees.

VEGETABLE CASSEROLE

2 cans mixed vegetables, drained
1 can water chestnuts, drained
1 cup chopped onion
1 cup mayonnaise
1 cup grated cheese

Mix all ingredients and pour into casserole. Top with crushed Ritz crackers. Bake at 350 degrees for 25 minutes.

PECAN PIE

3 eggs, beaten
½ cup sugar
¼ cup butter, melted
1 cup dark corn syrup
Dash salt
1 teaspoon vanilla
1 tablespoon cornmeal
1 cup pecans

Slightly beat eggs. Add sugar and butter, stirring well. Add syrup, salt, vanilla, and cornmeal. Stir well. Add pecans and pour into unbaked pie crust. Bake at 350 degrees for 50 minutes.

This is brother Haywood's favorite cake. I bake one and take it any time there is a family gathering at holidays, or family reunions.

OATMEAL CAKE

1¼ cups boiling water
1 cup quick oats
½ cup vegetable shortening
1 cup light brown sugar
½ cup light corn syrup
2 eggs
1½ cups flour
1 teaspoon soda
½ teaspoon salt
½ teaspoon cinnamon
½ teaspoon nutmeg
½ teaspoon vanilla

Preheat oven to 350 degrees. Pour boiling water over oats and set aside. Cream shortening, brown sugar, and syrup. Add eggs, one at a time. Stir oats real well and add to creamed mixture. Sift flour, soda, salt, cinnamon, and nutmeg. Stir vanilla into creamed mixture. Then gradually add dry ingredients. Mix well. Bake in 13 x 9 x 3-inch pan for 45 minutes.

TOPPING

1 stick margarine
1 cup brown sugar
1 cup shredded coconut
1 cup nuts, chopped
½ cup crushed pineapple, drained
½ teaspoon lemon juice

Mix margarine, brown sugar, coconut, and nuts. Put over low heat until melted. Add pineapple and lemon juice. Mix well. Pour over cake as soon as cake is taken from oven. Place cake back into oven on lower rack. Turn on broiler. Broil for about 15 minutes or until coconut begins to brown.

PEACH DELIGHT

2 (9-inch) baked pie shells
4 tablespoons peach gelatin
1 (8 oz.) package of cream cheese
1 cup water
4 large peaches (more if needed)
½ cup sugar
3 tablespoons cornstarch
1 cup sugar

Mix ½ cup sugar and cream cheese. Spread on pie shells. Put sliced peaches on cream cheese. Mix 1 cup sugar, cornstarch, and water. Cook until thickened. Stir in peach gelatin and let cool. Pour over peaches. After this is set, put whipped cream on top.

Jewell V. Atkins

Black Mountain, North Carolina

JEWELL V. ATKINS *is that rare person found in large families today, an unmarried woman who is an angel of mercy for her family. Let a sister or nieces and nephews, a brother, or an in-law have illness or death in the family, and Jewell is the first one on the scene. She scrubs and cleans, cooks and washes up, and helps in a thousand unobtrusive ways. A short, plump woman, Jewell has a big smile and loves to laugh and joke with people.*

My name is Jewell V. Atkins. I was born on May 11, 1924, at Pensacola in Yancey County, North Carolina, just ten miles from the county seat of Burnsville.

I can remember a long time back, you know, and one of the best memories I have is sitting in my mother's lap. She did not do handiwork while I was in her lap like she did with some of the other babies. I was a handful I guess. I helped on the farm because I always liked outside work the best.

Daddy grew corn, tobacco, potatoes, wheat, rye, oats—just about everything back in those early years. He would sell potatoes, sometimes a little corn. He sent the rye and oats to the water mill where they crushed them to make feed for the livestock. He'd get big old empty boxes from the mill, and he'd mix the oats and rye all up to feed the cattle and hogs.

He would have the wheat ground. The Greenville Milling Company from Tennessee would deliver their flour to stores in our community, and they would pick up our wheat and take it back to Greenville and bring us back flour that would be just like you'd get out of the stores. They'd send twenty-five to thirty cloth bags weighing twenty-four pounds each, which would be packed upstairs in the apple house.

The apple house? When we were children at Pensacola, there was a two-story building across from our house; it was next to a creek that ran down there. My father built big apple bins in the first floor, and stored wheat, rye, and oats after harvest. That's how come it got to be called the apple house. There was room for a couple of beds, and everybody wanted to sleep there because it was next to the creek. It had a metal roof, and it was especially nice when it rained. You could stay up late at night in the apple house and carry on as long as you wanted, and Mother and Daddy couldn't hear you.

We always had two or three milk cows, chickens, hogs, horses, and mules that did all the plowing and things like that. We raised beef cattle and our own pork and chickens. There were two hundred acres of land there counting the timberland. We'd farm approximately twenty-five acres each year.

Dad hired some outside labor now and then, but the most part was done by us at home. There were always extra hands at harvesttime. Everything was done by teams of horses and mules. The wheat, rye, and oats were harvested by an old-time cradle with a blade on it. The threshers would come and strip the grain out of the straw. Mother would spend days getting ready for them; there would be six to ten men to feed each day. I always looked forward to this time but Mother dreaded it each year, because it was so much extra work for her and us girls.

We cooked a lot of everything: ham, chicken, all types of vege-

tables, jellies, jams, cakes, and pies—they ate a lot. I had to help
Mother during those times and at holidays, but the rest of the time I
was outdoors as much as possible.

I finished high school in April of 1941. World War II broke out in
December, so shortly after that, I came to Swannanoa like most of
our family did. I went to work at Beacon Manufacturing Company. I
worked there for five years; we were busy making army and navy
blankets and also lend-lease blankets for Russia. We worked overtime
on Saturdays. During this time I stayed with my sister, Kate, and her
husband, Haywood, at Swannanoa. After that, I stayed some with
Mack and my oldest sister, Jeanette, at Black Mountain, but then
Daddy got sick, and I had to go back to Pensacola to help out for
awhile.

After that I got a job in Burnsville at the Duplan Corporation.
They had a weaving plant there; I was a weaver. We made all types of
dress fabrics. . . . I worked in Burnsville for five years, until the
company went out of business. Then I didn't work for a year—that
was in 1955—but in 1956 I went to American Enka Corporation
where I worked in the same department for twenty-seven years until
May 18, 1983, when I took early retirement at fifty-nine years of age.

My family always came first with me. When anyone was sick or in
trouble, I was always able to be with them. In fact, I stayed with Jack
while his brother, Grover, was born. I remember Mack came in about
daylight one morning and said that during the night he'd taken
Jeanette to the hospital and she had a baby boy. I helped Nette (as we
called her) for awhile after she brought the baby home. That baby
peed more than I ever saw a baby do before! I called him Andrew
Geyser after the geyser at Old Fort, across the mountain. It seemed
every time I started to diaper him he'd cut loose right straight up into
my face.

I have taken care of my sister Barbara countless times when she has been ill. She has two children, Ronnie and Karen, who are just like my own. Now each of them have children of their own; I love them to death. My only full brother, John Jr., died in 1968. He stayed with me off and on over the years. He was a very troubled young man: could never seem to find peace no matter where he was.

I would say I've been real happy here in the mountains of western North Carolina. I go to Florida to visit my sister Louise. I don't more than get there until I'm wanting to come back. I just don't like flat country where you can't see the hills. Another thing I like is the four seasons of the year. If you've missed one, you've missed them all. I like spring and the fall. After a hard winter everyone is ready for a new life themselves. In the fall the leaves are so pretty; it's the time of harvest and there's canning, freezing, and getting ready for winter.

I bought a house in West Asheville. I lived there fifteen years—while Daddy was still alive. He and mother both got ill and could work no longer, and they both came to live with me. Daddy died on August 3, 1960. After that it was just mother and me. She was able at that time to stay by herself part of the time; my niece, Joyce, stayed with us part time; that helped me.

Then Mother required full-time care. I bought a trailer and moved it next door to my sister, Emily, in Black Mountain. She worked part time, I worked full time, but between us we managed to care for Mother. Kate and the rest of the family helped out, also. But somebody had to be with her all the time. Finally I had to retire . . . and take care of her myself.

Eventually the time came when she needed more care, and we had to find her a nursing home; which we did. We all took turns going to spend a day with her after that. She was a very old lady when she died.

What are my favorite foods? Well, that would be hard to say, but milk and corn bread, all kinds of vegetables, and meat. I never cared for sweets. I like to cook sometimes. I never cared for handiwork at all, not even sewing on a button! I like outside work in the yard or garden. I love to can and freeze. I don't mind cooking; used to cook a lot more than I do now, I guess, because a lot more people used to come by for meals. Everybody has got so scattered now. I always keep soup on hand.

No, I don't have any certain foods I especially like to cook. I cook macaroni and cheese. I used to make spaghetti that the family talked about so much I got famous! Brother Gary keeps wanting me to make it again, but I haven't for a long time. Mostly I just cook plain old food. I don't do fancy dishes. I have high blood sugar and have to watch what I eat these days.

BUTTERMILK CORN BREAD

1 cup cornmeal
⅓ cup all-purpose flour
¼ teaspoon soda
1 teaspoon baking powder
1 teaspoon salt
1 egg, beaten
1 cup buttermilk

Preheat oven to 400 degrees. Mix dry ingredients than add egg and buttermilk, mixing well. Pour into a greased 8- or 9-inch iron skillet. Bake for 20 minutes or until lightly browned. Yields 6 to 8 servings.

OLD FASHIONED CORN BREAD

2 tablespoons shortening
½ teaspoon baking soda
½ teaspoon salt
1 cup buttermilk
¼ cup plain flour
¾ cup cornmeal

Melt shortening in medium-size iron skillet in 450 degree oven. Stir baking soda and salt into buttermilk. Add flour and cornmeal. Then add melted shortening and stir well. Let skillet get sizzling hot then pour in batter. Bake at 450 degrees for 15 minutes until top is light brown. Bottom will be much browner. Turn bottom side up. Cut into wedges and serve hot.

COLESLAW

4 cups cabbage, shredded
½ cup celery, finely sliced
¼ cup green pepper, finely sliced
¼ cup sweet red pepper or carrot, finely sliced
2 tablespoons green onion, finely sliced
¾ cup sour cream
3 tablespoons vinegar
3 tablespoons sugar
1 teaspoon salt
⅛ teaspoon white pepper
1 tablespoon celery seed

Combine cabbage, celery, peppers, and onion. Combine remaining ingredients; pour over cabbage mixture. Mix lightly. Yields 6 servings.

FRIED STEAK AND CREAM GRAVY

1 (3 lb.) sirloin tip roast or round steak, cut into ½-inch slices
1 to 2 teaspoons salt
½ teaspoon pepper (freshly ground is best)
1 tablespoon white vinegar
3 cups all-purpose flour

CREAM GRAVY

3 tablespoons all-purpose flour
2 cups milk
½ teaspoon salt
¼ teaspoon pepper

Pound meat into ¼-inch thickness. Cut each slice crosswise into 3 pieces. Place in large bowl and cover with water. Mix salt in the vinegar and marinate for 2 hours. Combine flour and pepper in plastic bag. Add meat (do not pat dry) a piece at a time and shake to coat. Heat oil in deep large skillet over medium-high heat. Add meat in batches (do not crowd) and fry until light brown, about 30 seconds per side. Drain on paper towels. Place meat on warm platter and set aside. You may tent with foil to keep warm. Pour off pan drippings, reserving 3 tablespoons. Add ¼ cup flour to drippings; cook over medium heat until bubbly, stirring constantly. Add 2 cups milk, cook until thickened, stirring constantly. Stir in ½ teaspoon salt and ¼ teaspoon pepper. Add steak to gravy; cover, reduce heat, and simmer 25 minutes. Remove cover, and cook an additional 5 minutes. Yields 8 servings.

SHUCK BEANS

Soak 2 cups dried shuck beans (leather britches, or shucky beans) in water overnight. Drain water and rinse beans well. Put beans in a 4-quart kettle and cover with water. Add a ham hock or ¼ pound seasoning meat. Cover and cook slowly until beans are tender and dry (may need to add water during cooking to prevent scorching, but beans should be dry when done). Salt and pepper may be added if seasoning meat is not salted.

BAPTIST PIE

1 can condensed milk
½ cup lemon juice
1 can pineapple tidbits
1 can mandarin oranges
1 can sliced peaches
1 large container whipped topping

Mix condensed milk and lemon juice until thick, add drained fruit, and fold in whipped topping. Pour into graham cracker crust and chill until firm.

Rossie Wagner
Bluff City, Tennessee

ROSSIE WAGNER *is in her early seventies. We sit in the dining room of her house at Cherokee Park, in Bluff City, Tennessee. Her house sits on a large lot; there is a garden down the slope behind the house. The front and sides of the yard are landscaped. Rossie is a widow; she is friendly, with a hearty laugh.*

I was born in 1914, in a large family and reared in Yancy County, at Pensacola, North Carolina. I was one of four children [from] my mother's first marriage; my father died at thirty-two years of age, when I was three years old. Later Mother married a man with children, and they had children. Therefore, there were three sets of children. We lived on a farm where we grew most of the food we ate. We had a good time together.

We worked hard and were lucky if we could go swimming on Saturday afternoons. But we gathered at neighbors' houses from time to time, where we peeled apples, stringed beans, or helped at a molasses stir-off, anything to have a chance to socialize a little with friends.

There were more girls than boys in the family, so the girls had to go out on the farm and work just like the men did. Momma did most of the cooking; as we grew older she let us do some cleaning.

Jeanette was the oldest of Mother's first set of children, then came

96

Gary, me, and Kate. Jeanette used to whip me all the time, because when Mother would leave her something to do, which she didn't want to do, she'd try to make me do it for her. (Ever notice how the oldest child always tries to be boss when the mother is not around?) I recall one time though when she got a whipping when Mother got back because I told on her. Mother whipped her for whipping me. We did so many things back then it would fill a book.

My brother Gary and I always fussed at each other a lot, too. We would argue about who was going to do things. One time Mother sent us up in the woods with a bag to rake up dry leaves. I don't remember what we were getting them for, but we went after the leaves and he wanted me to hold the bag. Then he didn't like the way I was holding it and started fussing at me. I threw the bag down and told him I wasn't going to help him. I started to run, and he ran after me saying he was going to whip me. I knew that he would if he caught me. Trying to get ahead, I ran through some blackberry briers and got scratched all over. I was running as fast as I could when I looked back to see how close he was. There was a black snake after me! The snake was scaring Gary, too, and he stopped. I started screaming and I guess that scared the snake. I don't know what happened, I probably outran it. Gary ran in the opposite direction!

During the depression I came to Swannanoa and got a job at Beacon Manufacturing Company, working for $3.50 a week—that was just before Roosevelt became president. When the New Deal came into being under Roosevelt and he signed his new labor law, they had to pay $12.50 a week. I thought I was going to be wealthy.

I was an inspector in the factory. I had to look at the weave of the blankets and see what defects there were and correct them. I worked there about ten years. I was fifteen or sixteen when I started to work. Then I got married to Harold Boone and we moved to Asheville to live. From there we moved to Bristol, Tennessee. We lived there three or four years before our marriage broke up, and I was left the sole support of our twins—Jim and Marje.

I got a job at Big Jack Manufacturing Company as a part-time office worker, and then I'd go to the cafeteria and be cashier during the lunch hour. At the end of the day shift at four o'clock I'd go home and then come back at six to open up for the second shift. We lived close by the cafeteria, and my boss was kind enough to let me bring the children with me, and they did their studying in the cafeteria. The children and I quite often ate our evening meal at the cafeteria.

Ten years passed, then I met Charlie Wagner and we got married. I stayed home a little while, but I wasn't happy at home because I had worked all my life. I got a job at the H. P. King Company for a couple of years in retail sales. Later I went to a Sears and Roebuck store, as a decorative consultant—they sent me to school to learn and I worked for them ten years.

My life seems to go in ten-year cycles!

The children had left home by that time. When I got tired of working at Sears I stayed home for a few months. Later I got a job at Miller's Florists in Bristol, as a general office clerk and bookkeeper, and I worked there for eleven years; then it was time for me to retire. I told the manager I'd retire that fall. Before then Charlie got sick, and I had to stay home with him. We had just bought this big house here in Cherokee Park. It required a lot of upkeep and it was hard taking care of that and Charlie, too. After being in and out of the hospital for awhile, Charlie died. It was lonely after he died. I found myself thinking more often about parents and childhood days; memories like that seem clearer now than they were twenty years ago.

You want to talk about food? Well, a typical breakfast was usually bacon or sausage, perhaps an egg and toast. There would be milk and coffee. Sometimes we might just have cereal. I made a point to always have an evening meal for my children, especially when they were in school and I was working. That was our special time of the day. Even if I had beans and potatoes, it was important to prepare that meal and serve it as attractively as I could for the children. We would sit around the table and eat, and we had a lot of fun just sitting and talking. After we'd get up, we all might go in different directions, so that was a special time for us.

I never liked housework. I love to work out in the yard and the garden—but not the house. I did my own sewing when the children were small; I made all their clothes and most of mine. I made plenty of mistakes during those years. What mother does not look back and say she would have done things differently if she had known what she knows now?

Spending time with children seems to be a lesson that parents never learn by other people's experiences. I would find more time to spend with my children; I would let other things go about the house—which I learned in later years didn't have to be done. The sad thing is you have no way of ever going back. It's like the water running down here in the stream; you can't step in the same water twice.

I was a better housekeeper back then than I am now. I thought everything had to be done on schedule each day. At that time, holding down two jobs—because that was our only income—I still felt I had to do everything I could. We were living in a rented apartment but it was home to me, and I tried to make it look as attractive as possible.

I did all the cooking when the children were growing up. I've collected a lot of recipes over the years—more than I can even think of ever using. I only raise a small garden since Charlie has been gone; I make pickles each year but seldom do any canning. I love my flowers and like to spend a lot of time with them. In the wintertime I do needlepoint and make quilts.

In the past I was involved with volunteer work. I was in the Red Cross during World War II as a nurse's aide, then served a year as a Gray Lady. During the last twenty-five years I've been very active in the Business and Professional Women's Club. I belong to a garden club. Outside that, I guess my chief interest is playing bridge. I belong to a bridge club and we play twice a month. I enjoy that. It gets me out of the house and with other ladies that I enjoy being with. We take turns meeting in different homes. Sometimes we'll have a dessert bridge. I try to stay active.

You know if you want to keep young, stay busy and don't sit down. I've never heard of work killing anybody. If you can get the proper rest at night, then you can hold out to stay busy during the day. Through the years I've had bad situations to face. Raising two children by myself at times was a problem and a burden. But you never solve a problem by sitting down and feeling sorry for yourself. There'll be a way if you try, and the busier you stay, the better off you are.

I'm getting older now, but there's lots of things I still want to do. I want to travel and now that I am retired I am planning to take some trips.

I have picked some recipes which are unusual in some way. The first one is a very old recipe for a Christmas drink . . . but I have added a few modern items.

WASSAIL

1 gallon cider
1 large can pineapple juice
1 (6 oz.) can frozen orange juice
1 quart water
6 tablespoons lemon juice
2 cups sugar
6 to 8 sticks cinnamon
60 whole cloves

Heat sugar and water to boiling point. Add spices tied in bag. Simmer 20 to 30 minutes. Mix and add juices. Heat together. Remove spices. Wassail may be stored several weeks in refrigerator.

EASY ROLLS

6 tablespoons shortening
¼ cup sugar
1 teaspoon salt
1 cup boiling water
1 package yeast
¼ cup lukewarm water
1 egg
3½ cups flour

Mix together shortening, sugar, salt, and pour boiling water over mix. Stir until dissolved. Sprinkle yeast on lukewarm water and mix. When first mixture cools, beat in egg and dissolved yeast. Stir in 3½ cups flour. Cover and refrigerate. Roll out and cut into rolls 1 hour before baking. (Rolls are best if dough is refrigerated overnight.)

CREAM CHEESE CONGEALED SALAD

1 (15 oz.) can crushed pineapple
1 (8 oz.) package cream cheese
1 large box gelatin, any flavor
1½ cups cold water
Large container whipped topping
Nuts if desired

Bring pineapple and sugar to a boil. Add cream cheese and stir until melted.
Add flavored gelatin and cold water. Let set and add whipped topping.
(Sometimes I add coconut and almond extract to recipe.)

SALMON PÂTÉ OR BALL

1 (15 oz.) can salmon, drained
1 (8 oz.) package cream cheese, softened
2 tablespoons chopped green onions
1 tablespoon lemon juice
½ teaspoon salt
⅛ teaspoon pepper
½ teaspoon dill seed
2 tablespoons capers

For Pâté: In blender or food processor blend first seven ingredients until
smooth. Spoon mixture into small bowl; stir in capers. Cover and refrigerate
for about 2 hours. Serve with crackers.

For Ball: Omit dill and capers, add ½ teaspoon liquid smoke. Shape into
ball. Roll in 3 tablespoons parsley and ½ cup nuts.

HOT CHICKEN CASSEROLE

1½ cups cooked chicken
1 cup diced celery
3 tablespoons minced onions
1 can cream of chicken soup
¼ teaspoon salt
¼ teaspoon white pepper
⅓ cup mayonnaise
½ cup slivered almonds

Combine ingredients in baking dish. Bake at 350 degrees for 1 hour. Serve over mounds of chinese fried noodles and garnish with hard-boiled eggs.

TENNESSEE BUTTERMILK CAKE

1 teaspoon soda
2 cups sugar
1 cup margarine
4 eggs
2 cups flour
1 teaspoon baking powder
¼ teaspoon salt
1 teaspoon vanilla extract
1 teaspoon lemon extract

Cream together sugar and margarine. Add eggs one at a time. Dissolve soda in buttermilk. Add baking powder, salt, and flour. Add to creamed mixture. Stir in extracts. Bake at 325 degrees for approximately 1½ hours, or until done.

A friend gave me this adapted recipe with the remark that it was, "Rich enough to be a sin." I always call it "My Sin."

MY SIN DESSERT

1 stick margarine
1 cup self-rising flour
1 cup chopped pecans
1 (8 oz.) package cream cheese
2 cups whipped topping
1 cup sugar
2 small packages of butter pecan with almond Jell-O pudding
2½ cups cold milk

First Layer: Put butter in glass baking dish and melt in 300 degree oven. Mix flour and nuts and put over melted butter, and mix lightly until flour is moist. Press down tightly. Bake at 300 degrees for 15 minutes. Let cool completely.

Second Layer: Have cream cheese at room temperature. Add one cup whipped topping and sugar. Spread on first layer.

Third Layer: Thoroughly mix Jell-O pudding with milk. Fold in second cup of whipped topping. Sprinkle with bittersweet chocolate or nuts. Keep cold until served.

BRIDGE PIE

1 small can lemonade concentrate
1 can condensed milk
1 (4-oz.) container frozen whipped topping

Beat all ingredients together until thick. Fill a baked pie shell. Chill. Serve with whipped topping.

IMPOSSIBLE COCONUT PIES

Grease and flour 2 (9-inch) pie pans
4 eggs, well beaten
1½ sticks butter, softened
1¾ cups sugar (or a little more)
1 teaspoon vanilla
½ cup self-rising flour
2 cups milk
1 (7-oz.) can flake coconut

Add butter to beaten eggs. Stir in vanilla, flour, and milk. Add coconut. Divide mixture to fill 2 pie pans. Bake at 350 degrees about 25 minutes or until golden brown.

Nick and Marje Owen
Bluff City, Tennessee

I WAS SPENDING *the night with Rossie Wagner in Bluff City, Tennessee. After a wonderful dinner, she and I walked through the subdivision to Marje and Nick's house. Marje is Rossie's daughter. We were greeted and ushered inside. We told them that I was interviewing people to find out about their lifestyles and the kinds of food they ate along with how it was prepared and any social connotations attached to food and food ways. Rossie suggested I talk with Nick first.*

My name is Nicholas Fain Owen. I was born in Bristol, Tennessee, and currently live in Cherokee Park, Bluff City, Tennessee. When I was a child we lived in a big old eleven-room, two-story house. I was the runt of the litter in our family of twelve children, three of whom are younger than me. There were five boys and seven girls. We all had nicknames. My nickname was Dodie. A sister near to me in age couldn't say Nicholas and called me Dodie. The name stuck. We went through one phase where everyone was known just by their initials. The boys fought a lot, and Dad would just order us to go out into the backyard and fight it out.

You can imagine Mother trying to feed us all. Breakfast was my favorite meal. It was always bread, country sausage or bacon, and eggs. All the baking was done at home. It was a treat when we had light bread. The boys learned to cook breakfast for themselves when they slept late. The next to oldest brother, whom we called Kewpie, was quite mean. . . . We had a coal stove and Mother kept missing her bacon and eggs each morning for awhile. She started banking the fire so we could not cook at night. [When a fire is banked, ashes are put on top of fire to smother out the flames. Coals stay alive deep under the ashes. When a fire is wanted, the ashes are raked back and the coals coaxed into flames again.] About two o'clock one morning she woke up and smelled bacon and eggs cooking. Knowing there was no fire, she went to investigate. Kewpie had turned her electric iron upside-down in a crock and was frying bacon and eggs!

Dad went to the store once a week. . . . In addition to a carload of groceries, he'd bring home about eight loaves of light bread. Since it was a treat for us, everybody went for it. Eight loaves lasted for about a day and a half. We raised hogs and grew our own wheat which was ground into flour. We raised most of what we ate on the farm. The children worked the farm after school, and through the summer. Mother never seemed to have time to make biscuits, but she baked what we called flat bread. She just pressed the dough out in a big pan and cooked it in a sheet. She put the flat bread on the table and one could just break off as big a piece as he needed.

We had a big pantry about twelve-feet deep and six-feet across. Dad would buy apples and oranges and stuff at Christmastime and Mother would put them in the icebox. She kept the icebox locked, otherwise we would have brought in our little friends and cleaned out a bushel of apples in nothing flat. We had an aunt, Mary Shanks, well, not really an aunt, but we all called her Aunt Mary. She stayed with us and helped Mother. She and Mother both had a key to the pantry. Well, stuff began disappearing out of the locked pantry. Mother said, "Mary, I know you're not taking stuff, but what on earth is happening?" Aunt Mary said, "Well, I wasn't going to say anything because I didn't want to cause any trouble. Let me show you something." Kewpie had slipped in and unlocked the window at the end of the pantry. He built him a ladder, and he'd come up and in the window and carry food out to the kids. Well, that window got nailed up and Kewpie got nailed, too.

Our house was never locked as a rule. We started staying out later at night as we got older. One time Dad decided he was going to put a stop to our staying out late, so he got a key to lock the front door. "At midnight, the door's going to be locked," he said. The first night it was locked, he caught Kewpie when he tried to sneak in at a window. It went pretty good for about three days, everyone was in by midnight. Then Dad had to go to Marion on business. At midnight Kewpie locked the door. Dad couldn't get in. The next day the lock was taken out of the door.

My oldest sister married James Conway Caine of Asheville, and his family always dressed for dinner: shirt, tie, and jacket. She brought him home, the first time, and at mealtime everybody came to the table that could get there. We always had two tables. So Conway asked Nell, "Where's the bread?" She says, "Right in front of you." He says, "How do I get it?" She says, "Just reach in there and break you off a hunk." After that he loved to eat at our house. It was rather stiff at his house.

We had a big table with a bench on either side and a chair at the head and at the foot of the table. Dad sat at the head and Mother sat at the foot. We older Children sat on each end of the benches. The younger ones, the first ones to eat at the first table, had to sit in the middle of the benches. So when we heard, "Dinner's ready," or "Supper's ready," all the young kids would start running so they could sit in the middle. If you didn't make it to the middle you had to wait for the next table.

The first ones would eat, the table was cleared and reset for the second table. This was done at every meal in our house. Poor Mother! She cooked breakfast and cleaned up and started dinner (which was in the middle of the day) and cleaned up, and it was time to start supper. Somewhere between times she did the laundry and ironing. Of course, some of the girls helped.

The boys worked with Dad. He was the hardest boss I ever had in my life. We worked with him after school and through the summer. He was a contractor. If we weren't on a job, then we were on the farm. The farm was at Walker Mountain. When we went to work for Dad, we did everything from the digging of foundations to the topping of a chimney. He said he wanted us to have more than one trade to fall back on. We had to do it all, and we had to do it well. Mostly I ran the floor sander, and asked one of my friends to switch jobs with me: he to run the sander and me go out on the construction work. He said fine. The head foreman said, "Give this boy the biggest pick and shovel you got and put him to work." He did. One day of digging foundations and I was ready to go back to the sander!

But I learned the trade. I can make and build things. We never have to pay a repairman for plumbing or electrical work or anything like that. There's a lot I don't know, but there's not a whole lot I won't try.

Two of my brothers loved to hunt. There was quite a bit of woods out on Walker Mountain. One brother would have been happy to have lived out there. One time before I was born, the house was quarantined for scarlet fever; he was out in the woods. When he came home, Mother told him to go to Grandmother's. He headed for the woods instead and stayed there while Mother thought he was at Grandmother's, and Grandmother figured he was at home. He spent the entire quarantine out in the woods.

When I grew up, I started out working as an auto mechanic for an uncle who had a garage in Norfolk, Virginia. I came back home for a weekend visit and when I went back somebody had stolen all my tools. So I left and came to Bristol, Tennessee, where I got a job in the post office. When I first went to the post office, I never meant to stay. The postmaster decided she was going to get rid of me; I decided she was not. By the time the fight was over I had in ten years and couldn't afford to quit.

I was hired to be a letter carrier. I served three rural routes for awhile, but the last few years I carried a business route downtown. Along rural routes they put the flag up if there is mail they want you to take back to the post office for them. This one lady had a mailbox that opened at the top instead of the front. One day the flag was up, so I reached in to get the mail—and I didn't know what I'd run my hand into! It turned out to be a piece of chocolate pie. Very good, too.

One time I'd just taken over a new route. I walked up on a lady's porch. She came out and said, "Do you have time?" I'm scratching my head, wondering what the previous carrier had been up to. I said, "I beg your pardon?" She again said, "Do you have time?" I said, "Time for what, lady?" She said, *Time Magazine.* When she realized how her question had first sounded, she put her hand over her mouth and fled back into the house.

I used to deliver lots [of mail] addressed "Occupant." One piece of mail I delivered had a space between the *o* and the first *c.* I left it. The lady in charge of the mail said, "Mr. Mailman, you left the wrong mail. There's no O. C. Cupant lives here."

Did I ever cook? Well I have done a little bit every now and then. I make mayonnaise biscuits. You only need mayonnaise, buttermilk, and flour. Since I had a heart attack, we don't eat fried foods anymore. Marje has been learning all kinds of new recipes for low-fat foods. Some taste pretty good; Marje fusses if she catches me in the kitchen fixing eggs. Mother ate bacon and eggs every day, sometimes two or three times a day, and she lived to be ninety-six years old. My father drowned when he was fifty-eight. They died on the same day thirty-five years apart.

Father had been at Mendola with some friends fishing, and across the river a girl fell in the water. She couldn't swim. Dad swam across and got her to the bank where they could stick a pole down and she got hold of it. Dad didn't make it back across the river. He'd given blood the day before, and perhaps that weakened him. Mother was presented the Carnegie Award because Dad had saved the girl's life.

Everybody called Mother "Snowdrop." Her grandchildren called her "Granny Snow." One of my sisters said to Mother one day that if she got any fatter she would melt like a snowdrop. In our family that's all it took to give Mother a nickname. She was short, about five feet four inches tall and she weighed about 190 pounds. When she was in her eighties she went to our family doctor. He said, "Snowdrop, you're not on the farm anymore. You don't work like a field hand, but you're eating like one. You're eating too much. It's bad for your health."

"Well, I could quit eating and live another ten to twelve years, or go ahead and eat and just get four or five—well, if it's all right with you, I believe I'll just go ahead and eat." Mother proved the doctor wrong—I guess she had good genes.

Mother was a good country cook. Do you know Tennessee Ernie Ford who used to sing? Well he lived around the corner and he loved to come up when Mother was fixing a pot of brown beans and a pan of corn bread. He'd come up and eat cold beans and corn bread after school.

The first recording Ernie Ford made was "Mule Train," when he become famous. His parents [had] sent him to the Chicago Conservatory of Music, to study to sing spirituals. They nearly died when he came out with "Mule Train."

Ernie's father worked at the post office. Ernie's mother used to take us kids up in the Knobs for a bacon bat. We cooked out up on the knobs. We'd take our food and skillets and build a little fire, cook whatever we brought. No, I don't know why they called it a bacon bat, but it was always called that. One time Mother was asked to help chaperon a group of young people. They got up on the knobs, got their fire built, and the boys and girls started pairing off. The other lady said, "Mrs. Owen, let's go round 'em up and bring 'em in." Mother said, "Oh, let's leave 'em alone and let 'em spark a while."

Mother was a great one for using the old home remedies. One time Marje called her and said, "Snowdrop, guess what? Lee's cutting her first tooth." Then I heard Marje say, "Vicks salve and nutmeg?" Then I knew Mother had thought Marje said, "Lee's got the croup," because she always rubbed us with that mixture when we got the croup. Talk about a weird smell! The nutmeg was for opening the sinus cavities, she said. Vicks salve and nutmeg was almost as bad as the spring tonic we had to take. Every spring we got sulfur and molasses for a tonic. It was supposed to purify your blood. I know one thing—after that, anything else tasted good.

One time Kewpie fell and cut an awful bad gash on his leg. Hack, the oldest brother, wrapped it up the best he could and brought him home. Mother unwrapped it, packed the wound full of sugar and lard, and wrapped it back up again. It healed and didn't even leave a scar.

I think Mother's favorite remedy was concocted to keep me from cutting school by saying I was sick. She caught on to that pretty fast, and would say, "Well, if you're sick, you'd better have some castor oil." After a dose or two I was convinced she meant it. Mother used to say I was the best baby she had. Well . . . I was just smarter. She didn't catch me out like she did the others.

Let me tell you about Rebecca Gay, one of my sisters. She was just a little bit meaner than any of the girls. She was downtown with two of the younger sisters, Edna and Wilma. Dad had given each of them a dime to get a sundae. They went to the drugstore and, while they were eating their sundaes, two well-to-do women got up to leave. One of them said, "I'll get the check," and the other one said, "No, let me get it."

Rebecca Gay said to her sisters, "You give me your money, and when we start out, Edna you say, 'I'll get the check,' and I'll say, 'No, let me get it.' And we'll act like big shots." So they got up to the cash register and Edna said, "Let me get the check." Gay said "Okay!" and took off out the door with the money. Edna and Wilma sat there and cried. The druggist knew Dad and called him. "I told them they could go on home and pay later but they won't leave." Dad went over and bailed them out. He got so tickled he never spanked Rebecca Gay either. Gay grew up and went to Miami to live and work. She married a man whose last name was Laughinghouse. Now, you know that it was fun to introduce her as Gay Laughinghouse!

When I introduced Marje to Mother, I said "Snowdrop, this is my new girlfriend, Ethelbert Gushingbottom." Mother giggled. I said, "Mother, don't laugh. Her father was a Cherokee Indian with diarrhea." she said "Ohhh!" I started off when she stopped. Mother had a sense of humor; I guess she would never have survived otherwise.

Mother seldom ever whipped any of the children. She said, "Wait until your Daddy gets home." She'd tell Dad. He'd make us go out and get a long switch, and he'd whip us. One time my youngest brother, Gene, had acted up a little, and Mother said, "Wait until your Daddy gets home."

Gene and I went to the basement just before it was time for Dad to get home. He put on two pairs of pants and we got cut grass and padded him good, hoping Dad wouldn't know the difference. I said, "Now you holler and scream when he whips you." So when Dad came in, Mother told him. He sent Gene after the switch, and he got a big one—he was over-confident—and Dad whipped him with it. Gene just hollered and cried. Then he came down in the basement and boasted, "Boy, I didn't feel a thing!" We were getting that grass out and taking that extra pair of pants off him when we looked up and Dad was standing in the door. Then we both got whipped, and we didn't even have one pair of pants on. I told Gene, "I'm never gonna help you again."

Gene was the most gullible child I've ever seen. One time he had a tooth come loose, and he wouldn't let anybody pull it. I could talk him into anything, though, and I said, "Let's tie a string around it and tie it to the doorknob. You just sit there and when somebody opens the door, your tooth will be gone and you won't feel a thing." But come to find out, I had him on the wrong side of the door! He lost three teeth. And I got another whipping.

Someone asked Mother one time which of her twelve children was her favorite. She said, "The one that's sick until it's well, and the one that's away until it's home."

We took a break. Marje served dessert and coffee and we chatted with Aunt Rossie for a little while. Nick stayed to help Rossie carry the dishes into the kitchen and wash up, while Marje and I went back into the den. Marje is a petite blond with brown eyes and very white teeth. Her voice is soft but her words are distinct.

My name is Marjorie Boone Owen. I was born in Asheville, North Carolina. I currently live with my husband Nick, in Bluff City. I have a twin brother, Jim. He lives in Richmond, Virginia. He has a daughter whose name is Marjorie Lee Boone. Of course I don't care for her at all! [Laughs]

When Jim and I were young, the evening meal was the most important part of the day at our home. We'd sit down at the table to eat and that was our time to be together. Mother worked, we were in school, so it was important for us to have some time together. We hashed out everything, the good, the bad, and enjoyed it. We would sit and talk long after we finished eating.

Favorite foods? Oh, a number of things. One of my very favorites was hamburger corn-pone pie. It's really good. Mother got concerned about us sometimes because we ate so much!

This has absolutely nothing to do with food, exactly, but it does have to do with keeping house. I was married for five or six years, I guess, before I realized that one could do housework on other days besides Saturdays! When we were growing up Saturday was the day we cleaned the house.

Every Saturday we were awakened with a list of what all we had to do that day. Every Saturday we washed the woodwork. We hated Saturdays. Mother even had what we called her Saturday dress—I wonder how many of those she wore out. She nearly killed us on Saturday. We just thought we were the most underprivileged children in the world. The things we had to do on Saturday, you wouldn't believe! But, you know, somehow every Saturday afternoon enough money was scraped together for us to go to the movies.

Now I just clean house whenever I have to. You know, I only found out after I was grown that Mother hated housework. She hated it! I thought she loved it because she was the cleanest person I know.

Jim learned to buy groceries. Mother taught him to buy and pick out the right things—to know a good buy when he saw it in the grocery store. He was very good with that. He got out of some of the

Saturday cleaning because of getting the groceries, but not all of it.

You could say I learned to cook by "using my judgment." Mother was always too busy to teach me to cook: What little I learned was from watching her do it. I would say, "Mother, how much of this or that?" She said, "Well, just use your own judgment." If she said it once she said it a million times. I said, "I don't have any judgment, Mother! How much?"

But you know, now I love to cook. I am happiest in that kitchen. If only someone would just take care of the rest of the house and leave me in the kitchen! I have lately had to watch my weight, and I'm real interested in fixing low-calorie things.

HAMBURGER CORN-PONE PIE

1 pound ground beef
1 small onion, chopped
1 can tomato soup
1 cup chopped green pepper
1 can whole kernel corn
½ teaspoon chili powder
Dash of pepper and salt
Corn-bread batter, 1 recipe

Brown ground beef and onion. Drain and add tomato soup, green pepper, and corn. Add ¼ cup water, chili powder, salt, and pepper. Simmer 15 minutes. Make favorite corn-bread batter and put into a greased and floured pan. Pour first mixture on top of corn-bread batter. Bake at 450 degrees for about 20 minutes or until crust is brown.

A quicker method: If you have leftover chili, use it and the corn bread recipe. Bake the same way.

JACK FARR'S CHIPPED BEEF DIP

1 small package cream cheese
1 cup sour cream
½ cup chopped celery
½ cup chopped onion
½ cup chopped green pepper
1 can chopped beef
½ tablespoon garlic salt
1 tablespoon horseradish
Pepper and dill to taste
2 tablespoons Worcestershire sauce

Cook in oven or microwave until bubbly. Sprinkle with pecans.

LEMON ROSEMARY CHICKEN

2 large chicken breasts, split and skinned
2 tablespoons margarine, melted
3 tablespoons fresh lemon juice
1 clove garlic, crushed or finely minced
1 tablespoon instant minced onion
1 tablespoon rosemary, crushed
½ teaspoon salt
Dash of coarse black pepper
Parsley or paprika

Preheat oven to 350 degrees. In a bowl, combine melted margarine, lemon juice, garlic, onion, rosemary, salt, and pepper. Arrange chicken in a shallow casserole or baking pan, and pour mixture over chicken. Cover and bake until tender—40 to 50 minutes—basting occasionally. Uncover casserole and bake 10 minutes longer to allow chicken to brown. To serve, sprinkle with chopped parsley or paprika.

SPEEDY SPAGHETTI SAUCE

12 to 14 ounces very lean beef cut into ½-inch cubes
⅓ to ½ cup water
2 beef bouillon cubes
1 envelope Italian or other herb dry salad dressing mix
1 (4-oz.) can sliced mushrooms, drained
1 (15-oz.) can whole tomatoes (sliced or quartered)*
1 medium green pepper cut in ½-inch squares
½ teaspoon sugar

Brown beef cubes in pan sprayed generously with cooking spray. Add dressing mix, tomatoes, mushrooms, and beef bouillon dissolved in water. Simmer approximately ½ hour. The above may be done in advance and refrigerated. Ten minutes before serving, add sugar and green pepper. Serve over spaghetti, rice, or noodles.

*Use fresh tomatoes when available

SALMON NICHOLAS

1 (15½ oz.) can salmon, drained
1½ cups cracker crumbs
2 tablespoons lemon juice
1 tablespoon mayonnaise
1 egg
Cooking spray

Preheat oven to 450 degrees. Mix all ingredients together in large mixing bowl. Shape into 6 patties. Place on medium-size cooking sheet sprayed lightly with cooking spray. Bake at 450 degrees on one side for 10 to 15 minutes or until brown. Turn and bake 8 to 10 minutes on other side, or until brown.

MARJE'S ONE-DISH DINNER DELIGHT

6 (½-inch thick) pork chops*
½ to ¾ cup water
2 chicken bouillon cubes
1 or 2 vegetable bouillon cubes
3 to 4 medium-size potatoes, quartered or cut into 1-inch cubes
6 small whole carrots**
4 to 6 small whole onions
2 large stalks celery cut into 1-inch pieces
1 (16 oz.) can green beans, drained
1 (15½ oz.) can whole tomatoes, quartered (fresh is better)
Dijon or brown spicy mustard
Sweet basil
Mrs. Dash seasoning (with no salt added) or lemon pepper

Preheat oven to 350 degrees. Trim all excess fat from chops. Spread both sides of chops with mustard and sprinkle each side with sweet basil. Place chops in ungreased baking pan, 1½- to 2- inches deep. Dissolve bouillon cubes in water and pour around chops. Cover and bake 20 minutes. Remove from oven.

Place vegetables—except for green beans and tomatoes—around chops; sprinkle lightly with Mrs. Dash or lemon pepper. Cover, return to oven, and bake until vegetables are crisp-tender, 30 to 45 minutes. Remove from oven.

Add green beans and tomatoes to top of vegetable mixture. Cover and return to oven only long enough to heat through. Do not overcook vegetables. All except step four may be done in advance. Serve on a large platter.

*Substitute beef or poultry
**Substitute or add vegetables as desired

OWEN'S CHOCOLATE CAKE

⅔ cup shortening
3 eggs
1¾ cups sugar
2 cups self-rising flour
1¼ cups milk
1½ teaspoon vanilla
½ cup cocoa

Cream shortening. Add eggs and beat well. Add sugar and mix well. Add flour, milk, vanilla, and cocoa. Bake in 2 greased and floured 9-inch pans at 350 degrees for 30 to 35 minutes.

CHOCOLATE ICING

2 cups sugar
½ cup milk
½ cup shortening
¼ cup white syrup
¼ teaspoon salt
Cocoa as desired
1 teaspoon vanilla

Put all ingredients in pan and heat, stirring constantly, until mixture comes to a hard boil. Boil exactly 1 minute without stirring. Set on rack to cool. Beat until creamy and add vanilla.

Banner Elk Women
Banner Elk, North Carolina

Helen Baucom

Helen Baucom is a tiny woman who lives alone in a big gray house set back from a large front yard in Banner Elk, North Carolina. She has neatly curled white hair, wears delicate makeup, and her eyes sparkle as she talks about her garden, the women with whom she holds bake sales, her daughter Jane Ellen, and her family. Helen is eighty-two years old.

I was born in the small town of Ferguson in Wilkes County, North Carolina. My mother died when I was about three years old. Later on, my father had to go to Banner Elk on business and, while there, he met the woman who would become my stepmother. She was a Banner; her ancestors were the first settlers in Banner Elk. This place got its name from the Banner family and the many elk that roamed up and down the mountains and along the river. She and my father had one child, my half-sister who was as close to me as any sister could be.

We moved to Banner Elk when I was just eight years old. I was enrolled at the Lees-McRae Institute as a boarding student in the first grade. It was not a college at that time. I went to high school there also, and later when it became a college, I took some college courses.

When I was growing up, about the only social life we had was through the church. There were parties given by different ones every now and then. My father was very protective and didn't like for me to stay out late at night and was not happy when I did go to a party. Father was the postmaster, and when he became ill I had to work in the post office. However, he lived to be ninety-two. While working at the post office, I got behind in my college work.

While taking college courses, I met my future husband who was the business manager of Lees-McRae. He worked for the college for twenty years. So I went from being a student to becoming the wife of an administrator. That was interesting and challenging. We had one daughter, Jane Ellen.

My stepmother was a very good cook; in fact all the Banner women were good cooks. We had the traditional kinds of foods to eat every day and traditional things for Thanksgiving and Christmas, such as ham, turkey, or chicken.

Two of the earliest things I learned to cook were fruitcake and angel food cakes. My husband loved both, and I made hundreds of them during our married life. We always had a big garden and raised lots of vegetables to eat.

The joy of my life and what I did for recreation was to raise flowers. Right now I have a big dahlia garden in which I have about fifty plants. I have to dig them in the fall and replant in the spring. This year I had tuberous begonias on the porch and a long row of ornamental kale down the side of the yard—you probably noticed it as you came in.

I know you are interested in our group efforts to raise money for different projects. I think it is something that keeps us going; gives us something to think about and talk about instead of our aches and pains.

Some of us talk on the phone every day. People say we look and act younger than our age. The other day I had my hair fixed at the beauty shop. The operator said, "Oh, you got down before I let the chair down!" Well, I didn't know the chair let down! It wasn't any bother for me; I just jumped down. I am not going to be helped around until I am helpless and can't do anything about it. Nellie Ramsey and I run around together. We visit. We belong to the same church, and they put us on visiting committees and things like that.

Yes, we each have special things we like to fix. We each bake and sell our speciality. For example, Prudence, a lady who lives here, makes the most delicious lemon pies. People come to the sales early hoping to get one of Prudence's pies.

We try to attach our bake sales onto something else which is more likely to have crowds of people. Once or twice we sold baked goods at the Wooly Worm Festival and the craft fair they have in the fall.

You never heard of a Wooly Worm Festival? Well it's held over here in the field at the college auditorium. Both kids and grownups gather and bring in woolly worms. They've got strings that go up so high and you put your woolly worm down here and then you have to stand back and let them climb the strings and whichever gets to the top first is the winner. Then they choose all those that get to the top to be in a big race, The one that gets to the top first is the big winner that day. Then the mayor takes the wooly worm and examines it and tells the audience what the coming winter will be like.

I have been a widow for many years. My husband had his first heart attack when Jane Ellen was in high school. He died a few years later. . . . I never have time to be lonely, though, because Jane Ellen and her family, my flowers, my friends, and the bake sales all keep me busy. Some of my friends fuss at me and say I work too hard. But as Nellie says, you've got to keep going as long as you can. And if you can help a worthy cause while you keep occupied, that's the best way of all.

REFRIGERATOR ROLLS

2 cups milk
¼ cup sugar
½ cup shortening
1 package yeast
5 cups flour
1 teaspoon baking powder
½ teaspoon soda
1 teaspoon salt

Scald milk, sugar, and shortening. Add yeast to 2 tablespoons milk mixture. Add 2½ cups flour, stir and let rise 1 hour. Add 2½ cups flour which has been sifted with baking powder, soda, and salt. Mix and put in refrigerator. The next day make into rolls and let rise until double in bulk. Bake at 350 degrees. I roll out dough and cut with biscuit cutter. Then I dip each roll in melted butter and fold over in half.

MILKY WAY CAKE

4 Milky Way bars
2 sticks margarine
2 cups sugar
4 eggs
3 cups plain flour
½ teaspoon soda
1¼ cups buttermilk
1 teaspoon vanilla
1 cup chopped nuts

Melt candy bars with 1 stick margarine. Set aside to cool. Cream sugar and other stick margarine; add eggs, beating well after each. Sift together flour and soda. Add flour mixture and buttermilk alternately to creamed sugar. Add vanilla and nuts. Last of all add the melted candy. Pour into greased and floured tube pan and bake at 325 degrees for 1 hour or until tests done. Glaze with any chocolate glaze or icing or serve plain.

COCONUT POUND CAKE

6 eggs
1 cup shortening
½ cup butter or margarine
1½ cups sugar
½ teaspoon almond extract
½ teaspoon coconut extract
1½ teaspoons baking powder
3 cups sifted cake flour
1 cup milk
2 cups coconut—fresh grated or canned flakes (I grind the canned coconut)

Preheat oven to 300 degrees. Grease and flour 10-inch tube pan. Separate eggs, placing whites in large bowl, yolks in another large bowl. Let egg whites warm to room temperature for at least 1 hour. With electric mixer at high speed, beat egg yolks with shortening and margarine until well blended. Gradually add sugar until light and fluffy. Add extracts and beat well. At low speed, beat in flour alternately with milk in thirds, beginning and ending with flour. Add coconut and beat until well blended.

Beat egg whites until stiff peaks form. With wire whisk or rubber scraper, gently fold whites into batter until well blended. Pour into a greased and floured 10-inch tube pan. Bake 2 hours at 300 degrees, or until cake tester comes out clean. Cool in pan for 15 minutes. Remove from pan. Before serving, dust with confectioners' sugar or glaze top and sprinkle on coconut.

Beulah Puckett

It was the fall of the year in the North Carolina mountains. I had come to Banner Elk with Jane Ellen Stephenson to interview her mother and a group of women who spent a lot of their time organizing and holding bake sales for charitable projects in the region. Jane Ellen, wife of the Berea College president, had told me about them and invited me to go with her for a visit to her mother, Helen Baucom.

Helen had arranged for the women in her group to come at different times through the evening to talk with me. Beulah Puckett was the first. She came into Helen's living room with brisk movements and speech. We shook hands and she settled back into an armchair looking at me expectantly.

I am Beulah Puckett. I've lived here in Banner Elk since I was two years old—which is seventy-nine years. I am eighty-two years old. We moved here from Watauga County. There were seven children in my family, and we had plenty to eat. We didn't have a lot of meats and things like we do today, but we kept two cows and chickens. We kept a hog, of course, and for breakfast we would almost always have eggs, gravy, meat, and hot biscuits. I went to Valle Crucis boarding school for four years of high school. Then while I was in school over there I got a chance to go to England and France as a nurse for an eight-year-old child. We were there from May to September. I went with this lady from Nashville, Tennessee. I came home and got married in November of 1928.

My husband's name was James Puckett and we had three sons. My husband died when he was only forty-four. It was very hard. By that time James Junior was married, Wayne was in the navy, and Lawson was fourteen years old. I worked in a lunchroom ten years and worked in the hospital more than eighteen years. I retired when I was nearly seventy-four. . . . But I'm still working!

I help with the fair that we have at Valle Crucis. This year was our sixth fair. I make twenty-four pints of apple butter each year for the fair. It sells for $3.50 a pint. I also help with a quilt that we make and raffle off each year. All proceeds go to Avery and Watauga Counties. The hospital in each county has received $2,000 from our group. And we've given to the Girl Scouts here and the animal shelter and the spouse abuse center. We take in around $8,000 at the fair, but we have some expenses.

The money goes for good causes. When we first started we had everybody save their milk jugs and made cider right on the grounds up there. They used a hundred bushels of apples this year. My brothers are picking some more. They will make apple cider all day long. The women will make apple butter in a big brass kettle. They made over a hundred pints last year, and it was real good apple butter. They are also going to have barbecue. They have the best barbecue and Brunswick stew for lunch. Well, people eat all day long! Then at the elementary school they will have the supper. At seven o'clock we have a square dance in the apple barn. I'd get home around midnight. But now it's getting to be too much for me.

Yes, making apple butter is a specialty of mine. I can't tell you exactly but I've got the apples and a big heavy kettle which belonged to my mother. It holds about two-and-a-half gallons of apples, and it makes about ten pints. No, I don't do much cooking aside from the apple butter; I stay busy and don't do much cooking. I have a bowl of cereal in the morning with bananas. . . . Then for lunch I'll eat a sandwich and a bowl of soup. In the evening I'll cook a good meal of vegetables—you see I eat plenty. Different people have said they thought that's the reason I stay as well as I do, because I eat so well. A lot of old people don't eat well when they live by themselves. I stay busy and eat sensible meals.

I have a few recipes here I used to make for family and friends. I just can't cook as much as I used to do. I guess cooking is like driving a car, you never forget the motions!

OVERNIGHT POTATO CASSEROLE

8 to 10 potatoes
½ cup melted margarine
¼ cup chopped chives
1 clove garlic, minced
1 (8-oz.) package cream cheese
1 (8-oz.) carton sour cream
2 teaspoons salt
Grated cheese

Peel and cook potatoes until tender. Drain and mash. Soften cream cheese and beat well with electric mixer until smooth. Add potatoes and remaining ingredients, except cheese. Mix. Put into greased baking dish. Cover and refrigerate overnight. Remove from refrigerator about 15 minutes before baking. Uncover and top with grated cheese and bake at 350 degrees for 30 minutes.

CRANBERRY SALAD

1 cup boiling water
1 package cherry gelatin
1 cup orange juice
½ cup celery, chopped
¼ cup pecans or walnuts, chopped
1 small can crushed pineapple, drained
1 small can cranberry sauce or ½ of large can

Mix cherry gelatin in boiling water and stir well. Add orange juice, celery, pecans or walnuts, crushed pineapple, and cranberry sauce. Mix well and put in refrigerator for several hours before serving.

WILMA'S PUNCH

2 quarts apple juice or cider
3 cups orange juice
1 cup brown sugar
Dash cloves
Dash nutmeg
Large dash cinnamon

Mix well and serve hot.

EASY COCONUT CAKE

1 box white or yellow cake mix
1 can cream of coconut
1 can condensed milk
1 (9-oz.) container whipped topping
1 can coconut

Prepare cake mix as directed on box. Bake in 13 x 9 x 2-inch cake pan. Remove from oven when done and punch holes in cake with a fork while still hot. Pour condensed milk over cake, letting it soak in. Then pour the cream of coconut over it, letting it soak in. Cover with whipped topping and spread the coconut over it. Keep leftover cake in refrigerator.

MY FAVORITE CHOCOLATE CAKE

⅔ cup shortening
3 eggs
1¼ cups sugar
1¼ cup milk
2 cups self-rising flour
1½ teaspoons vanilla
½ cup cocoa (optional)

Cream shortening, add eggs, and beat well. Add sugar, milk, flour, vanilla, and cocoa. Beat well and pour into 2 round cake tins. Bake at 350 degrees for 25 to 30 minutes.

CHOCOLATE ICING

2 cups sugar
½ cup milk
½ cup shortening
¼ cup white syrup
¼ teaspoon salt
1½ squares chocolate or 3 tablespoons cocoa
1 teaspoon vanilla

Put all ingredients in pan and mix well; heat mixture and stir until it comes to a hard boil. Boil exactly 1 minute without stirring. Put on rack to cool, then stir until cool, adding vanilla.

Nellie Ramsey

My name is Nellie Ramsey. I am a native of Banner Elk, North Carolina. The other place I've lived is in Portsmouth, Virginia, where my husband worked at the Navy Yard. After that we moved to Tennessee where he worked with the TVA. I am seventy-five years old.

I had always wanted to take nurse's training. I wanted to take training when I finished high school and before we married. He said, "No." He said, "Those girls aren't nice." He said, "We'll just break up if that's what you want to do." I went on and got married, but I still wanted to be a nurse all those years. When our son was in the last year of high school my husband went back to Norfolk to work.

While he was gone, a man I'd met at Lee's McRae College came to see me. His father was in the hospital. He wanted me to sit with his father, and I did. But my husband came home and caught me. He was not happy about it. I stood up to him and said I was going to take training no matter what he said. He wanted me to go to Norfolk with him; I wouldn't give up on my goal. My son and I stayed there and he went back to Norfolk. I finished training and went to Raleigh for my state boards. I was forty-two years old. Then we went to Norfolk. We lived there seven years. I came back here and worked at the hospital until I retired when I was sixty-two.

You want me to talk about our bake sales? It's been about ten years since we started. There is a group of us older people who know each other because we live in the same community and go to the same churches and things like that. One thing we had in common was we all are good cooks and like to bake. At first we didn't have any organization or anything. We just started having sales because one day someone said the rescue squad and the fire department needed some new equipment. We just sort of arrived at the idea of having a bake sale to help raise money. We had bake sales, we had rummage sales—all to raise money. Sometime after that we had a sale to help raise money for the hospital. Last year we paid for a birthing bed at the hospital. One time we raised money for an air conditioner on the psychiatric ward. We also made quilts to be raffled off.

After the first one or two bake sales, we felt we needed more organization to be efficient about the sales. Now when we decide to have one, I get on the telephone and call the women. I tell them we're having a bake sale to raise money, and I tell them what it's for. I ask them to help bake something for the sale. I tell them to bake more than one thing, that just cookies or brownies aren't enough. Cakes sell for more. Most of our cakes sell for around $10, and some bring as much as $12. Of course the size of the cake and how fancy it's decorated determines the price. What sells best that I bake? I guess my coconut cake.

We usually average around $600 at each sale. We have raised lots of money for bigger things, and it's a good thing to do especially when you're old. When you're getting too old to put one foot in front of [the other], as they say, and you keep going in spite of that, it's good for you. If you sit down and give up you are gone.

Some of us are in our seventies; a few in their eighties. We have a good time. . . . The things I treasure most in my kitchen right now are my cookbooks and my mixer. I am always on the lookout for new recipes. Some people say when they find something good they just stick with that. I don't do that. I try different ones and I'll take them to church suppers to see how people like them.

I hope I never do like Flossie did one time. She carried two pies to the bake sale we had down here at the fire department. She got her crusts and put chocolate filling in and put meringue on top. You know, she forgot to bake those crusts first.

I took my Social Security at sixty-two, but I said if the Lord lets me live I'm going to keep going. If you retire and sit down and fold your hands you are not going to live long. Some people tease us about our bake sales. Helen told me a cute joke the other day; I think Jane Ellen told it to her.

It seems that this group of old women died and Saint Peter said the premises were a little crowded at the moment and they would have to wait somewhere else for a little while. So they went below to wait. Finally one day the devil called up St. Peter and asked were the rooms yet ready for the ladies? He then said, "You've got to take them out of here. They've been having bake sales and have almost raised enough money to buy an air conditioner!"

We have around twenty-five women involved one way or another in the bake sales. Most of them are regulars and most of them do one special thing. Some of the women are so good that people reserve their specialities from one bake sale to the next.

APRICOT NECTAR POUND CAKE

3 cups sugar, scant
1 cup shortening
6 eggs
3 cups flour
¼ teaspoon soda
½ teaspoon salt
1 cup sour cream
½ teaspoon rum extract
1 teaspoon orange extract
1 teaspoon vanilla
½ teaspoon lemon extract
½ teaspoon almond extract
½ cup apricot nectar

Grease and flour large tube pan. Cream shortening and sugar. Add eggs, one at a time, beating thoroughly. Sift together flour, soda, and salt. Combine sour cream, flavorings, and apricot nectar. Add alternately flour and sour cream mixture, and mix until blended. Bake in preheated 325 degree oven about 70 minutes.

COCONUT CAKE

1 box white cake mix
1 teaspoon coconut flavoring
Mix cake according to package directions. Add flavoring, and pour into 3 (9-inch) greased and floured cake pans. Bake 15 to 20 minutes.

OLD-FASHIONED BOILED FROSTING

3 egg whites
3 cups sugar
⅛ teaspoon salt
1½ teaspoons white vinegar
1½ cups water
1½ teaspoons coconut flavoring
1 teaspoon cream of tartar
Pinch of salt

In small bowl, let egg whites warm to room temperature. In medium pan, combine sugar, salt, and vinegar with water. Cook over medium heat stirring until sugar is dissolved and syrup is clear. Continue cooking over medium heat without stirring to 245 degrees on candy thermometer.

With mixer at medium speed, beat egg whites until soft peaks form when beater is slowly raised. Add cream of tartar and pinch of salt. Mix on high speed and gradually pour hot syrup in a thin stream over egg whites, beating constantly. Add coconut flavoring and continue beating until stiff peaks form when beater is raised and frosting is thick enough to spread.

"The original boiled frosting recipe did not call for cream of tartar, but I find it makes the frosting creamier. Do not scrape pan when you cook the syrup for egg whites."

CUCUMBER PICKLES

4 cups sugar
4 cups vinegar
½ cup pickling salt
1¼ teaspoons turmeric
1¼ teaspoons celery seeds
1¼ teaspoons mustard seeds
Small cucumbers
3 onions, sliced thin

Mix ingredients, but do not heat. Fill containers with cucumbers and onion. Stir syrup well and pour over the mixture. Refrigerate for 5 days before tasting. Will keep in refrigerator for up to 9 months. Yields 6 pints.

ONION CHEESE MUNCHIES

1 (8-oz.) package cream cheese
1 tablespoon grated onion
1 tablespoon mustard
1 egg
Plain soda crackers

Let cheese soften to room temperature. Add other ingredients and whip thoroughly. Spread over crackers, being careful to cover crackers. Place crackers on cookie sheet. Toast under broiler for a few minutes, or until cheese turns light brown. Serve warm.

PARTY HAM BISCUITS

2 cups flour
¼ teaspoon salt
2½ teaspoons baking powder
3 to 4 tablespoons shortening
¾ cup buttermilk
½ teaspoon soda

Cut shortening into flour until mixture is like meal. Combine milk and soda and stir in flour mixture, blending well. Roll dough to ¼-inch thickness and cut with a small cutter. Place on lightly greased pan. Bake at 500 degrees for 7 to 8 minutes. Wrap in towel. Slice open and spread lightly with butter. Cool. Place thin slices of ham in biscuits. Bake at 450 degrees for 4 to 5 minutes. Makes 2 dozen.

SALMON LOAF

1 can salmon
3 cups hot mashed potatoes
2 tablespoons margarine
½ cup hot milk
1 teaspoon chopped parsley
1 egg, well beaten
Season to taste

Mix and place in greased baking dish. Brush with milk. Bake in a moderate oven until brown.

EGG PASTRY FOR FRIED APPLE PIES

3 cups flour
1 teaspoon salt
1 cup shortening
1 egg, beaten
4 tablespoons water
1 teaspoon vinegar
Salad oil to make 1 inch in frying pan

Combine flour and salt, cut in shortening until mixture resembles coarse meal. Combine egg and water; sprinkle over flour mixture. Add vinegar and stir lightly until mixture forms a ball. Wrap in wax paper. Chill for 1 hour. Makes pastry for 1½ dozen 5-inch fried pies. Roll ⅓ of pastry out at a time, and cut with 5-inch saucer.

Put 3 tablespoons apples on ½ circle and fold over. Wet fingers to seal pies. Use fork dipped in flour to press edges together. Heat salad oil in frying pan to 375 degrees. Fry until golden brown, turning once.

Marietta Breidenthal

The next woman was born in St. Louis, Missouri, the child of German-descent parents. Her husband grew up in Kansas City, Missouri. They came to North Carolina shortly after their marriage.

My name is Marietta Breidenthal. My husband and I moved to Banner Elk just before Halloween in 1956. He was a doctor and came to serve at the hospital here. He and Dr. Lawson Tate were the only two doctors here, serving a seventy-bed hospital. Our three daughters were born and reared here—true Carolinians. Two of them went to the university at Chapel Hill and the other one went to Wake Forest College in Winston-Salem.

In 1956 there were not many outsiders coming to the area. The first Sunday we were here we went to church and soon started singing in the choir. Eventually my husband played the organ and directed the choir. I felt we were received well. The community was small and close-knit. The local people invited us to family affairs and other things that went on.

What I ate as a child was different from the way people here eat. My grandparents came directly from Germany, so we had a lot of German dishes; German potato salad, for instance. People around here don't know how good that is. I think the mountain people have more English and Scottish backgrounds and thus have recipes based somewhat on their heritage.

I participate in the bake sales we have at the hospital here but not to the extent that Nellie, Beulah, or Helen have. I also have worked at our volunteer sales at the hospital. . . . One recipe that I have made for years is called Blueberry Yum-Yum. I've made it so many years I've forgotten where I got the recipe. I've changed it a little, as most cooks do, I suppose.

I like to cook. I like to learn shortcuts though so that I don't spend so much time in the kitchen. One I learned recently is to use Bisquick to make sesame seed sticks. Bake and eat. That's the kind of baking I do the best, I suppose.

SESAME SEED STICKS

Bisquick
Butter
Sesame seeds

Make bisquick according to directions for biscuits. Roll out and cut into long sticks. Dip each stick in melted butter and put in pan. Sprinkle on sesame seeds. Bake and eat.

BLUEBERRY YUM-YUM

CRUST

16 graham crackers or 1 cup crushed
2 tablespoons brown sugar
⅓ cup sugar
⅓ cup margarine

Crush graham crackers and add sugars. Melt margarine and blend. Arrange in pie plate and put in freezer to chill.

FILLING

2 beaten eggs
1 (8 oz.) package cream cheese
½ cup sugar

Cream the cheese and blend in the sugar. Add beaten eggs and continue beating. Spread on crust. Bake at 350 degrees for 20 minutes (or until knife inserted comes out clean).

TOPPING

1 can blueberry pie filling or 1 quart blueberries
¾ cup water
1 cup sugar
3 tablespoons cornstarch
1 tablespoon orange juice

Simmer 1 cup of the berries in ¾ cup water 3 to 4 minutes. Combine 1 cup sugar and 3 tablespoons cornstarch and add to the cooking berries, stirring all the while until the syrup is thick and ruby clear. Stir in 1 tablespoon orange juice. Put the remaining 3 cups of berries on the baked pie, and then pour the cooked mixture over all. Chill the pie thoroughly before serving. Serve with whipped cream or ice cream on top. Sometimes I pipe a decorative edge of whipped topping around the pie.

Note: Since we have lots of huckleberries on our land, I frequently use them instead of the blueberries.

Esther Lowe

The next woman to be welcomed by Helen was Esther Lowe. Very precise in her speech, delicate and well-dressed, she sat perfectly at ease.

I am not going to tell you how old I am; you see Helen here doesn't know. I would not mind you knowing, but not her! I was born in Ashe County, in a small town called West Jefferson.

I went into nurse's training which was a three-year course. . . . I worked for a year after I finished training in the Ashe County Hospital—I work at the health department now. I met a man from Banner Elk, we got married, and have lived here ever since. I was twenty-eight years old and had never cooked a meal.

My husband helped his father here on the farm at Banner Elk. We lived with my mother-in-law for several years and I didn't do any cooking but did start learning to bake. The first roast that I ever did kept burning and burning. I called my husband in a panic and asked what I should do. He said, "Take it off the stove!" Stupid wasn't it? But that's how little I knew back then. You know, it just thrills me to death when I bake something that's better than Helen's—especially when she's given me the recipe! When we have the bake sales I don't bake things, I buy them! I'm not the baker, I am the buyer!

Helen bakes this Milky Way cake that is simply wonderful. One time a bake sale was being held for the Humane Society. I needed a cake badly because I was having unexpected company and no time to bake. I called Helen and asked to buy that cake. She made me drive the seven miles to where the sale was taking place, pay them there for the cake, and drive all the way back. I think she should have just let me have it here and turned in the money! But she said if everybody did that there'd be nothing for the bake sales.

When I go into my kitchen to bake anything, if there is anything dirty, I've got to wash that up before I start. . . . I'm different in that way from Helen. She just goes into her kitchen and pushes things back, and the way she bakes is all over the kitchen. There's flour on the floor, there's flour over the counter, and honestly it's the biggest mess ever was. How things turn out to be so good, when she is so messy, I just can't understand!

OATMEAL JUMBLES

1 cup shortening
1½ cups brown sugar, packed
2 eggs, well beaten
6 tablespoons milk
3 cups oatmeal
2 cups flour, sifted
1 teaspoon cinnamon
2 teaspoons baking powder
1 cup chopped nuts
1 cup raisins

Cream shortening. Add sugar, eggs, and milk. Beat this mixture then add dry ingredients which have been sifted together. Add oats, nuts, and raisins. Bake at 350 degrees.

BLUEBERRY MUFFINS

1 egg
½ cup milk
¼ cup vegetable oil
1½ cups sifted flour
½ cup sugar
2 teaspoons baking powder
½ teaspoon salt
1 teaspoon vanilla
½ cup blueberries, dusted with flour

Heat oven to 400 degrees. Grease and flour muffin pan. Beat egg; stir in milk and oil and vanilla. Put dry ingredients in with flour, and sift into milk mixture and stir until flour is moistened. Carefully fold in blueberries. Makes 12 muffins. (I always double this recipe.)

Jane Ellen Stephenson
Berea, Kentucky

I
T WAS NEAR *the end of a hot clear day. I rang the doorbell at*
the college president's house which was answered by the housekeeper.
She invited me in and about that time Jane Ellen appeared at the head
of the beautiful old stairway leading above the front hallway. Jane
and John Stephenson live here along with their three children. I went up the
stairs and into Jane's study where we prepared to talk.

I was born in Banner Elk, North Carolina, population about three
hundred all the time that I lived there. My mother had grown up
there. My father was from the Piedmont section of North Carolina
but came to Banner Elk to go to school. He became the business
manager of Lees-McRae College after graduation. I spent the first
nineteen years of my life there. I attended Lees-McRae Junior College for two years then transferred to the University of North Carolina at Greensboro. I had started college earlier than most because I
skipped the twelfth grade. I don't have a high school diploma.

There were four of us who, when in the eleventh grade, looked at
what was available for us to take in the twelfth grade. We had to go
by bus to the high school—seven miles each way—so when we
looked at what was left for us to take next year, besides senior English—which was the only requirement we needed—the only subjects left were things like physical education, chorus, band, and glee

club. We decided to take senior English at Appalachian State College [now Appalachian State University] and graduate. The high school principal was very upset and said he would not give us our diplomas. At that time principals frowned upon anyone who wanted to leave early because that cut their enrollment and their money by so much. That's when we decided to see if Lees-McRae would accept us without a diploma. After some tests devised just for us, they let us enter as college students. After finishing college work at the University of North Carolina, I taught at Lee Edwards High School in Asheville for a year and then came back to Banner Elk because my father died, and Mother needed help to manage his businesses. I got a job at Lees-McRae and, because they wanted their faculty to have at least a master's degree, I went on Saturdays and during the summer to Appalachian State University and worked on the master's degree.

Later on after marrying and living in Lexington, Kentucky, I got another master's degree at the University of Kentucky and was taking courses working toward a doctorate when we moved to Berea. I also worked at the University of Kentucky, developing special programs and services for adult students.

My memories of food? Well, Mother tells me that I didn't eat very well when I was little and was always underweight. She was always trying to get me to eat. I can remember her playing games and making the food look attractive so that I would want to eat it. When I got to be ten years old, she says, just suddenly I began to eat and gain weight all on my own. Mother has always thought food is very important and likes to feed people.

Father always had a garden in back of our house, and Mother canned vegetables and fruit. Later when freezers were available, she would freeze food, too. We had apple trees, and they would buy peaches from a truck from South Carolina or Georgia. All winter we enjoyed the wholesome things she'd canned. Father was a meat-and-potatoes person, and expected us to have meat and vegetables every day. He loved to eat.

I did not have any particular interest in cooking when I was a child. I wasn't interested in housework of any description! I liked doing what my father asked me to do better than what Mother did. Father taught me to type before I took it in school. I typed letters and bills and things for him. Really, I don't think Mother encouraged me to cook because she liked to do it so well.

When John and I got married I told him I couldn't cook. He said, never mind, he could cook. But I found out all he knew how to cook was pork chops and how to get soup out of a can. I could do bacon and eggs, a steak on a grill, and bake potatoes. That, along with a salad, was the extent of our eating at first. We lived in Banner Elk for awhile, and Mother took pity on us and invited us down for a lot of meals. We were married in March and went to Chapel Hill that following summer for John to do graduate work. That's when I started studying recipes and learned to cook.

Mother always stressed nutrition. I do the same things with my children although I don't worry too much about whether they're eating pizza or hamburgers or fast foods. I think there's some of that which can be nutritious and that it doesn't hurt to eat things like that once in awhile. I guess I don't center our lives around food, however. We should have a lot of occasions where you don't offer food.

When I was growing up we cooked everything. We never ate any raw vegetables except carrots and celery every now and then. Meat had to be cooked and cooked and cooked. I used to hate cauliflower because the only way I ever ate it was cooked. When I learned it could be eaten raw, that's the way we've had it ever since. There are many vegetables that taste better lightly steamed.

Probably the biggest differences in our likes and dislikes is that I don't cook much seafood or fish for John because I don't like it very much. That may be from growing up in the mountains and just not having it. When John was in college at William and Mary he had the chance to eat a lot of seafood. He also spent time one summer on an island in Canada, and I think he had lots of seafood then, too. Of course we had mountain trout. I will eat some fish, but as far as shrimp and octopus and squid and all those things that he likes, I can't even bring myself to cook them.

At home a typical meal would have been a roast with gravy and mashed potatoes. Corn, either cut off or still on the cob, green beans, applesauce, tomatoes, and cucumbers, and bread. Always homemade bread. Mother made wonderful rolls, corn sticks, biscuits, and corn bread. We had some kind of corn bread at least for two meals a day. The rolls were usually served for the Sunday meals and always a cake or pie, or something real good which Mother had baked.

I just do ordinary meals to get us through. However, I like planning party foods, hors d'oeuvres, a tea, or a reception where you have a lot of little goodies, little cakes, or tarts or things made with cheeses. I prefer doing things like that to cooking meals perhaps because I can be more creative in that way.

We have a friend in Banner Elk who told us this past summer that her youngest daughter right after her freshman year in college, went to work at a very exclusive inn. She was supposed to be the salad and dessert person. She came home after two or three days there, all excited, and said, "Guess what, Mom, I learned how to make artificial Cool-Whip." Her mother said, "You did? How did you make it?" She said, "Well, you buy something at the store called 'whipping cream' and you just whip it and beat it and beat it and beat it and after awhile you've got artificial Cool-Whip!"

Our children had not had much butter until we lived in Scotland. Butter was cheaper than margarine there, and there was a bakery that made absolutely the most wonderful bread I've ever, ever tasted in my life. We had bread and real butter for every meal.

I had a real hard time weaning my family from using so much salt on their food. I have started reading labels carefully, and it's surprising what they put in our food. I also try to cut down on fats.

Since John became president of Berea College, our meal times together have changed drastically. I have to schedule when we can eat around everybody else's schedule. Then there are so many dinners and banquets we have to attend. Sometimes one or more of us will have to eat alone at different places. We do not have control over our food intake in the same way that we did before we came here.

This is a nice house for entertaining. We love to have groups in, and entertain between two and three thousand people a year in our home.

In addition to being wife and mother, Jane Ellen wanted very much to be involved in some kind of work to help women in the southern Appalachian area. She has long been concerned about the literacy problems in Kentucky. She is also an enthusiastic champion for women's rights, and had worked with nontraditional students, older women who came to the University of Kentucky. She knew there were many other women who had little or no opportunity to help themselves.

She secured funding to organize a program on campus which would bring in women, all expenses paid, to experience life on a college campus. Jane named her program the New Opportunity School for Women. She put notices in all the local papers in Kentucky, North Carolina, Tennessee, Virginia, and West Virginia, inviting women from low-income families who had a high school diploma or equivalent GED certificate to apply. After all details were worked out, fifteen women came for the first session in June of 1987. They had classes in Appalachian literature, learned to write résumés, go for job interviews, and worked on campus in various labor departments. Jane then received additional funding so that there is now a winter session as well as the one in June. The New Opportunity School continues very successfully. Many of the women who have attended have gone on into college work. Others have found better jobs or more satisfying life-styles. It is safe to say that every woman who has attended a session has gone away enhanced in some way.

We serve tomato punch often for "before dinner" receptions when we serve vegetables, dips, and cheese balls.

TOMATO PUNCH

1 (48 oz.) can V-8 Juice
5 teaspoons lime juice
3 teaspoons Worcestershire sauce
1 teaspoon salt

Pour over ice in punch bowl. Serves about 10 people.

CREAM CHEESE BALL

2 (8½ oz.) packages cream cheese, softened
1 small can crushed pineapple, well-drained
2 tablespoons onion, chopped fine
2 tablespoons chopped green pepper
1 tablespoon seasoned salt
4 ounces chopped pecans (reserve some to roll the cheese ball in)

Combine above ingredients. Roll into ball. Roll in pecans and refrigerate overnight. Serve with crackers.

This one is from my Lexington friend, Diane High.

HOT CRAB COCKTAIL SPREAD

1 (8-oz.) package cream cheese, softened
1 tablespoon milk
2 teaspoons Worcestershire sauce
1 (7-oz.) can crab meat, flaked
2 tablespoons green onions, chopped
2 teaspoons toasted almonds

Combine cream cheese with milk and Worcestershire sauce. Add crab meat to cheese mixture. Add green onions. Turn into greased 8-inch pie pan or small baking dish. Top with almonds. Bake in 350 degree oven for 15 minutes or until heated through. Keep cocktail spread warm over candle warmer. Serve with crackers (have spreaders handy). Should be eaten as soon as cooked.

I developed the following to serve for luncheons. It will serve from 6 to 8 people, depending on the serving size. We usually serve it on a lettuce leaf along with deviled eggs, date-nut bread, and fruit slices.

CHICKEN SALAD

5 cups of cooked chicken breast chunks
⅔ cup sweet pickles
½ cup crushed pineapple, drained
½ cup slivered almonds
½ cup Miracle Whip salad dressing
½ cup sour cream
1 to 1½ teaspoons curry powder

Mix ingredients and chill well before serving.

The original recipe for this sausage casserole was given to me by Marge Cochran, a friend in Lexington. However, through the years I have changed it to suit our tastes.

SAVORY SAUSAGE

1 pound bulk sausage
½ cup finely chopped green pepper
¾ cup chopped onion
2 (2⅛ oz.) packages Lipton's chicken noodle soup mix
4½ cups boiling water
1 cup raw rice
½ teaspoon salt
¼ cup melted margarine
1 cup slivered almonds

Brown sausage in large skillet; pour off excess fat. Add pepper, onion, and sauté. Combine soup mix and boiling water in large saucepan. Stir in rice. Cover and simmer 20 minutes or until tender. Add sausage mixture and salt. Stir and pour into large greased baking dish. Sprinkle a few almonds over the top. Drizzle with melted margarine. Bake at 375 degrees for 20 minutes.

We like gazpacho in summer and winter. I use canned tomatoes so that it can be made quickly and at any season.

GAZPACHO

1 (16-oz.) can peeled tomatoes
½ green pepper, cut in small pieces
1 clove garlic, cut up
½ to ¾ peeled cucumber, sliced
6 olives
⅓ medium onion, cut in small slices

Mix ingredients in blender on chop setting only for a few seconds—just
enough to mix.

    Add to mixture:
3 tablespoons olive oil
1 tablespoon lemon juice
½ to 1 cup water (depending on thickness desired)
1½ teaspoons salt
½ teaspoon paprika

Mix in blender just until mixed. Refrigerate 4 hours or more in blender
container. Blend again briefly, just before serving. Serve in small bowls. May
be served over ice cubes if eaten immediately. Makes about 8 servings.

    This recipe was given to me thirty years ago by a friend, Barbara
Smith, in Asheville, North Carolina. We used to eat it at her house
on New Year's Eve. It is easy and different.

PEANUT PIE

20 Ritz crackers, rolled fine
½ cup sugar
¾ cup chopped roasted peanuts
3 egg whites, beaten stiff
¼ teaspoon cream of tartar
½ cup sugar
1 teaspoon vanilla

Mix cracker crumbs with sugar and peanuts. Beat egg whites until stiff, and
add cream of tarter, sugar, and vanilla. Fold cracker mixture into the egg
white mixture. Pour into greased pie tin and bake for 20 minutes at 350
degrees. Let cool. Top with whipped cream and grated bitter chocolate. Pie is
best served 3 or 4 hours after baking. May be refrigerated for this period.

This is a recipe you can make several days ahead of an event. It can also be frozen, still in pan. I got the recipe from my mother-in-law in Virginia.

GRAHAM CRACKER BARS

Cook the following for 2 minutes:
1 cup sugar
½ cup milk
2 sticks margarine
1 egg, beaten

Remove from heat and add to this mixture:
1 cup coconut
1 cup graham cracker crumbs
1 cup chopped pecans

Ice the top layer of graham crackers with the following:
¾ stick margarine
2 cups confectioners' sugar
1 tablespoon milk
1 teaspoon vanilla or almond flavoring

Store in refrigerator until firm. Remove from refrigerator 1 hour before serving. Cut in squares.

This is a favorite recipe that my children, especially David, make a lot. The children called them pink things but I'm sure they must have another name.

PINK THINGS

2 egg whites
¼ teaspoon salt
¼ teaspoon cream of tartar
¾ cup sugar
1 teaspoon vanilla
Pink food coloring

Beat egg whites with salt and cream of tartar until very stiff. Add sugar very slowly. Add vanilla and food coloring. Last of all, fold in 1 small package chocolate chips.

With a teaspoon, drop on greased cookie sheet. Put in preheated 375 degree oven and turn off heat immediately and leave overnight. Take out in the morning. Makes about 40 cookies.

This is my favorite recipe. I have been making it since we lived in Chapel Hill in the early 1960s when John gave me a recipe book put together by the Junior League of Chapel Hill. This recipe was submitted by Mrs. Terry Sanford, wife of a former governor. It is without a doubt the best cheesecake I will ever make.

CHEESECAKE

2 (8-oz.) packages cream cheese
¾ cups sugar
4 eggs, separated
1 teaspoon lemon juice
1 teaspoon vanilla
½ pint sour cream
2 tablespoons sugar
½ teaspoon vanilla

Blend cheese and sugar with electric mixer. Add egg yolks and beat well. Add lemon juice and vanilla and mix thoroughly. Beat egg whites stiff and fold into cheese mixture. Pour into glass pie pan lined with graham cracker crumbs. Bake at 350 degrees for one half hour.

Mix sour cream, sugar and vanilla. Spread over cheesecake while it is warm. Return to oven for 5 minutes at 350 degrees.

Note: Use the largest pie pan available or 2 store-bought graham cracker crusts.

I clipped this from a newspaper when we lived in North Carolina in the 1960s. I have probably adapted it a bit to best suit us.

CHOCOLATE DELIGHTS

½ cup butter or margarine
1 cup sugar
2 eggs
1 teaspoon vanilla
2 cups flour
1 teaspoon baking powder
1 teaspoon salt
1 (8 oz.) package chocolate chips
¾ cup chopped peanuts

Cream butter and sugar. Add eggs and vanilla, and beat until fluffy. Sift dry ingredients and mix thoroughly. Spread in 8 x 12-inch greased pan. Sprinkle with chocolate pieces.

MERINGUE

2 egg whites beaten until stiff
1 cup brown sugar
1 teaspoon vanilla

Add brown sugar and vanilla to egg whites and beat until smooth. Spread meringue over mixture in pan. Sprinkle with chopped nuts and press lightly into meringue. Bake at 350 degrees for 35 minutes. Cut into squares when cool. Must be kept in sealed container as they easily dry out.

This recipe was given to me by my Aunt Ann. This is the pound cake that John likes so much, and it's so easy to make. There is one problem with this recipe, however, it does not rise well in high altitudes.

AUNT ANN'S POUND CAKE

1 cup shortening
3 cups sugar
5 eggs
3 cups sifted flour
1 cup milk
1 teaspoon baking powder
1 tablespoon vanilla
1 tablespoon lemon or orange or almond flavoring

Mix shortening, sugar, and eggs on high speed of mixer. Add sifted flour alternating with milk. Add baking powder near end of mixing. Add vanilla and other flavoring at end on slow speed of mixer. Bake in a Bundt pan for 1 hour and 20 minutes at 325 degrees.

Note: For a soft, moist inside and crusty outside, take hot cake out of pan as soon as you can handle and wrap loosely in plastic wrap. In about 30 minutes, remove this wrap and cover tightly with new plastic wrap. Store in airtight container.

Wilma Dykeman Stokely
Newport, Tennessee

I HAVE KNOWN *Wilma Dykeman Stokely for many years. She is a well-known writer, lecturer, and teacher and has traveled extensively both on this continent and in Europe, China, and Africa. She and her husband, James Stokely coauthored three books, and, under the name Wilma Dykeman, she is the author of thirteen books of fiction, including her best-known book entitled* The Tall Woman. *She lives in Newport, Tennessee. James Stokely died of a heart attack in a garden not unlike the one in which they were married. Theirs had been a true marriage. They were honored and respected by almost everyone who came to know them. Wilma is one of the trustees of Berea College and comes to Berea frequently. We arranged for an interview one day when she was in town. She came to the college library, where I work, and we talked.*

I grew up in Asheville, North Carolina; my mother still lives there, and no matter how far away I travel I always return there. We lived in the country and that, of course, was a great blessing. This was in Beaverdam Valley just outside Asheville. . . . Now our road is called Lynn Cove of the Beaverdam Valley. I am so glad that my mother has seventeen acres there because I think we can keep it as a little oasis.

I attended the Grace School near the Beaver Lake area there on the north side of town. I started in the first grade and finished high school all at the same school. You had a real sense of identification with the teachers and the students. You can't do that any more. I had a good experience there. I learned a great many things, especially about social relationships. . . .

I never went to school with any of the black students, and the black part of Asheville was very separate from the white part of Asheville. I look back and know that I missed something important by not having that opportunity.

What we learned at Grace School was not all in books. You learned things about the way people live, some of the ways in which children communicate to you about their households. Then I would hear from my parents about the parents of some of the children at school. There was one family with five children who lived up on the mountain. The father died from pneumonia, and I remember Mother going up and spending a night, helping, nursing, and coming back to say we'd have to do something to help the family. This was my first introduction to poverty, and I was really grieved to know about it. The family needed all kinds of help. My parents helped in the sense of being good neighbors; there was no sense of largess or charity.

Everybody had a hard time during the depression. The banks failed. Everybody lost money. Two of the fathers of students at school committed suicide because they were associated with the bank failures.

Father wouldn't let us talk about it after the first discovery that the banks had closed, so I hid and was crying. Little gifts of money I had received from my aunts had been deposited in the bank. I'd taken it myself and handed it up to the teller . . . and now that was all gone. So I was crying back in the closet. Mother wanted to know why I was crying. "I'm crying," I said, "because all my money's gone that I've taken in to the bank." She took me down and told my father and he said, "Well, we're going to have no more crying and no more talk about this." He said, "We are all healthy, we have our home, we have this land to live upon, and we're not going to have any more crying. We'll get along some way." That was a great lesson to me. My father lived most of his life in New York. Dykeman is an old Dutch name. When Mother went to visit up north where Father's family lived, she was very observant about their food. She particularly liked the way the meats were cooked, especially the roasts. She adapted northern ways of cooking with her own southern mountain heritage. The blend was good. One of her special favorites (and it would be mine too if it wasn't so darned expensive) is the standing rib roast. She can get it just right so that it's rare inside and well done and crusty outside.

My earliest memories about food are the smells. I have always had an acute sense of smell, and I remember the wonderful smells in the house as my mother cooked. She thought that things should be made from scratch, as they say now in the advertisements. One of the smells that I still love and associate with home is the smell of bread, and the wonderful smell of the yeast rising. . . . I've always liked breads—the breads of the world. One of the things I admire about Europe is the great bread made out of the coarse grains.

I must have been in second or third grade when I came home from school and I was hungry. Mother had made bread that morning, and I went in and saw those three loaves. I took a pinch out of the middle, thinking nobody would notice. It was so good I took another pinch, and I ended up pinching a hole through just about the whole loaf of bread. When Mother sliced the loaf, here were these marvelous slices with a great big piece taken out! I don't think I was really punished for that, although I don't suppose I was praised for it, either. It was a kind of tribute to the bread.

There were other smells at our house that I enjoyed. My mother believed in authentic things. She did not like veneered furniture, she did not like things that were imitation—in rugs or anything else.

We had Navajo rugs in our house simply because Mother had discovered them on a trip out West and thought they were beautiful because they were handmade. They were real wool made by real people. We still have those rugs. I thought it would be better to have an imitation oriental rug, or something, because the Navajo rugs were not fashionable then, especially where we lived in the South. Today, of course they are great collector's items.

I mention that because the same thing held true with so many of the foods that she fixed. I remember the wonderful smell of apple butter and of the early apples in spring. We had a little jersey cow and I can remember the taste of the milk . . . that buttermilk with the little flakes of butter on it! I remember Mother made butter and it would have little beads of moisture on it, and nothing you can get today can begin to compare with that taste. She also made cottage cheese with a wonderful texture and flavor. It's quite an art to get the milk just right for the butter. If it's too warm, the butter is all white, has no flavor; and if it's too cold, the butter won't gather.

I'm glad I didn't know about cholesterol back then! I loved the thick cream to put on oatmeal in the morning with a little brown sugar or to put on top of some wonderful dessert. We liked cobblers for dessert, blackberry or raspberry or any kind of fruit or berries. Mother made the most marvelous pie crust. She still does; she's an absolute premier maker of lemon pie. I have watched her make lemon pies for forty or fifty years and I still don't even attempt one. I tried a time or two and it was a disaster. When Mother really wanted to surprise me . . . she made me a lemon pie.

I remember Mother making ketchup. I can still remember the smell on a summer afternoon as she cooked the ketchup with spices and ripe tomatoes. She had green bottles with the kind of old wire tops that wired onto these tall bottles. They sat down in a copper kettle. I cite all these things because they are all authentic things.

Nowadays we hear people bemoaning the fact that they have to rush home, and they stop at the deli and pick up something, or they get something at the frozen-food counter and then resent having to wait long enough for the microwave to cook it.

In my novel, *The Far Family*, I created a scene of the family at dinner. I've always been disappointed that critics never really interpreted this scene although they've examined many other scenes in the book. The family of five brothers and sisters is coming together again in a moment of crisis. A brother comes from New England, a sister from South Carolina. One sister, Ivy, had remained at home in the mountains. The way Ivy brings them together is through the things that she prepares for the dinner. She has a big pork roast, because one of the brothers has always liked pork roast, and she has the applesauce because one of them has always relished fresh applesauce, and the corn puddings, and the various things that they all liked. Then she has the coconut cake and boiled custard for dessert because their father had always liked a fresh coconut cake. I think that the ritual of food says a great deal about the ways in which a family was bound together. I was trying to show that food is not just a matter of staying alive. It's also a matter of relating to each other and to the land and to the world around you.

It is sad today . . . most of the young people who live on fast foods won't know the richness of fresh bread, the flavor of fresh country vegetables gathered in the garden and immediately prepared. It's like so much of our heritage that's lost. We're so accustomed now to smelling pollution, chemicals, artificial smoke, and the different things that assault our senses, that we aren't even aware of the smell of lilacs or the smell of green grass being cut or the smell of the foods that we're talking about. What a loss it is because those are the natural smells.

One of the things I've always liked is just plain old dried beans, what mountain people call soup beans—there's no kind of dried beans I don't like. Now, of course, Jane Brody and all the health people are telling us we must eat more dried beans because this is the best protein we can have. The head of every list I see for healthful proteins are the dried beans.

When I was at Northwestern University in Chicago, before I'd come home, Mother would say, "Now, what do you want me to fix that will be special when you come home?" I always said, "I want beans and corn bread and onions and buttermilk." You see, I was just an old country girl at heart. Mother is a wonderful cook, roast leg of lamb, other kinds of meats, and I think she was always a little disappointed that I didn't want something like that instead of the same old things.

Years later I was traveling in France and, as you know, provincial French cooking is great. Out in France I discovered the cassoulet, which is a marvelous dish that is based on beans. They fix it with goose or with pork or other kinds of meat, other flavors, other things. That shows me the kinship around the world of certain basic flavors and basic foods. Now when I don't want to horrify someone by telling them about dried beans and soup beans, I say, "Oh, well, you know, this is a French dish, a cassoulet, that we're having." Take a good cassoulet and serve crisp coleslaw with it, and to round the meal out, you have crusty corn bread. Oh, I'm making myself hungry!

Mother taught me to cook as I grew up and observed her doing so many things in the kitchen. I remember when I wanted to wash dishes and had to stand on a little stool to do so. It was exciting at first. But as Jean Ritchie, the ballad singer, says when she learned to work in cornfields at first she was just so pleased but after about two days in the rocky fields the shine was gone. I loved to dash in and try to learn about everything so I dashed in and said, "I want to help dry the dishes." I'm sure that after a couple of days the shine was gone.

James enjoyed discovering the flavor of different apples. He
planted dozens of varieties. We didn't have the commercial "apple
factory" farm with only one or two varieties that were red for eye-
appeal and tough for shipping. He planted and tended and grew
apples with care, the way he wrote poetry. And he ate them with
relish, the way he read books. I guess that's a fair recipe for the good
life, isn't it?

CASSOULET (VERSION I)

1½ pounds white beans (navy, pea, great northern, or marrow)
2½ cups water
10 small white onions
3 cloves
1 (13¾ oz.) can chicken broth (not condensed)
1 pound carrots, cut in halves or thirds
1 bay leaf
2 cloves garlic, minced
½ teaspoon black pepper
1 teaspoon salt
½ teaspoon marjoram leaves
½ teaspoon dry sage leaves
¼ teaspoon ground thyme
1½ pounds link sausages (smokes are great)
2 frying chickens, cut in serving pieces
1 cup thin-sliced celery
1 (16-oz.) can tomatoes
1 cup dry white wine

Combine beans and water in a Dutch oven or casserole. Let soak overnight.
Stud one onion with cloves and add to beans. Also add the chicken broth,
carrots, bay leaf, garlic, pepper, salt, marjoram, sage, and thyme. Bring to boil.
Reduce heat, cover, and let simmer 1 hour.

Meanwhile, brown the sausage quickly in a skillet, and set aside. Then brown the chicken on all sides in the sausage grease. Remove, and add chicken to bean pot. Sauté celery in leftover grease until just tender. Add tomatoes, their juice, and wine. Bring to a simmer. Empty skillet contents into pot. Cover and bake at 350 degrees for 1 hour or until chicken is tender. Add halved sausage, and bake, uncovered, another ½ hour or so, until juice is reduced and chicken is almost falling from bones. Yields 8 to 10 servings.

CASSOULET (VERSION II)

2 pounds sweet Italian sausage
2 pounds beef chuck, cut in 1-inch cubes
1 large onion, sliced
2 medium cloves garlic, minced
2 green peppers, seeded and cut in eighths
1 pound white beans, cooked
1 teaspoon basil
½ teaspoon salt
1 teaspoon paprika
¼ teaspoon pepper
2 beef bouillon cubes dissolved in 1 cup boiling water
¼ cup chopped fresh parsley

Brown sausage, cut in thirds, and place in a 2½- to 3-quart casserole. Drain grease from skillet, reserving 2 tablespoons. Brown beef in 1 tablespoon grease and add to casserole. Sauté onion and garlic in remaining 1 tablespoon grease until tender. Add green peppers and cook 1 minute longer, stirring. Add to casserole, along with the cooked beans. Sprinkle with seasonings and mix lightly. Add bouillon. Cover and bake in a 350 degree oven for 1 hour and 15 minutes or until beef is tender. Makes 4 to 6 servings.

I like this pound cake because it is rich enough to merit its name, and it's not rich enough to make you feel really sinful. You know, the secret of pound cake is to be sure it is done but not dry. That is why I never have quite the same temperature twice. I judge by the way it has browned and by the old straw method—when it comes clean from the cake, the cake comes out of the oven at once.

Some people add frosting to their pound cakes. I do not. My family does not like frosting, and my friends who enjoy a slice with tea or coffee or a glass of cold milk never seem to object to cake without icing.

SOUTHERN SOUR CREAM POUND CAKE

1 cup butter
2¾ cups sugar (I use a little less)
6 eggs
2¾ cups flour
½ teaspoon salt
¼ teaspoon soda
1 cup sour cream
1 teaspoon vanilla

Cream butter and sugar. Add eggs, one at a time. Sift dry ingredients. Add dry ingredients alternately with sour cream. Add vanilla. Beat until smooth. Oil and flour a tube baking pan. Bake at 350 degrees 1 hour and 20 minutes. Cool.

Larry and Phyllis Henson
Winston-Salem, North Carolina

L ARRY HENSON *married his childhood sweetheart, Phyllis, and they have one son, Rodger, now in college. They live in Winston-Salem, North Carolina. Larry is six-feet tall, has light brown hair, fair skin, and blue eyes. It was early on Sunday morning, the breakfast dishes had been cleared away, but Larry and I still sat at the table. I asked him to talk about his childhood in Beattyville, Kentucky, his education, and any special interest he had in producing and/ or cooking foods.*

Since our interview, Larry has completed an Executive MBA degree at Wake Forest University and was promoted to assistant vice president of data services. Phyllis has opened a bookstore, Angelica's Books & Things. While the store takes a great deal of her time, she still does consulting work for Marriott Food Services in nursing homes.

I am the director of the computer center at Wake Forest University. I received my bachelor's degree in math from Berea College and master of science and applied mathematics at the University of Missouri in Rolla. I'd like to move to a larger school someday, possibly into a position comparable to a vice president's level in computer science or data processing.

I was born in Lexington, Kentucky, but my parents lived in Stanton. Shortly after that Daddy was drafted into the World War II.

After he came out of the service, we moved to Beattyville in 1946. I lived there until I left to go to college. In the early years we lived in two places, one on the Booneville Road in a big old two-story house on a farm, setting on the edge of some woods with a stream and a little waterfall. I enjoyed playing in the stream and exploring in the woods when I could. We lived there until 1952, when Daddy bought a farm on the other side of Lee County. Both places were about three miles from town.

As far as the kinds of food or activities we had at that first place, I don't remember a lot. Daddy raised sheep, rabbits, chickens, and hogs, and I remember watching the sheep being sheared and the hogs being slaughtered in the fall. The stream that ran through the farm ran over a small cliff at the edge of the woods and formed a small pool. Although we had electricity and a refrigerator, we stored milk in the pool at times. I don't know whether the electricity was out or not. I remember my mother making cottage cheese. She would cook milk on the gas stove until curds were formed and then drained them in a white feed sack. We ate the cheese with salt and pepper.

I also remember her churning. She had a hand-cranked glass churn with wooden paddles. She would work the butter with a cedar paddle to get the liquid out, then she'd put the butter in a saucer and shape it into a disk and create a design around the top and down the sides with the paddle. Sometimes I would do the churning. Later on we got an electric churn.

My father, Hollis Henson, one of eleven children, graduated from Berea in 1936. Out of the eleven, five of them had some association with Berea College. Daddy was reared on a farm in Casey County. He received a bachelor's degree in agriculture and became an agricultural extension agent. After a short training period in Pike County, he was assigned to Powell County, where he met my mother. Mother grew up in Clay City, the second oldest of five children. She finished high school and took secretarial and business training.

I have four sisters and a brother who died when he was sixteen. My sister Linda went two years to Berea, then transferred to Eastern Kentucky University; Rebecca and Marilyn got their degrees at Berea, and Jane did two years at Lees Junior College and finished at Eastern Kentucky University.

As a child I liked to go wandering through the woods exploring, especially on Saturdays or Sundays. I would spend all afternoon by myself. At our house mother did all of the cooking. By the time I got to high school age I tried my hand at making cookies and brownies. I enjoyed that and still bake cookies every now and then. I was always precise with my measurements. I accuse Phyllis of never following a recipe, but, being a dietitian, she knows pretty much what will happen if she modifies a recipe.

I always had a taste for sweets. Grandaddy (Mother's father) always had to have something sweet with every meal: breakfast, lunch, and dinner. So I got my taste for sweets from him, I guess. Sometimes when we visited him and grandmother in Clay City, he would put butter on a hot biscuit and sprinkle sugar on it. I liked that very much. We had jams, jellies, and preserves. Grandaddy grew blackberries and grapes. Each summer we would pick blackberries, which Mother canned or ground and made into jam. I liked the seeds in the jam. She would also make a cobbler or heat the blackberries which we would eat over hot, buttered biscuits. Mother also made apple butter and sauce and several kinds of jellies. My mother made the best cinnamon toast. She would mix brown sugar and cinnamon into the butter and make a thick paste, which she spread on a slice of bread and put in the oven under the broiler. It had a sweet, caramel taste.

I remember having fried chicken, especially on Sunday. I loved half-runner green beans. I would split hot biscuits and spoon bean juice out of the pan on top—and it was good! We had roast beef, pork chops, and ham. If we ran out of home-cured meat, my parents would buy meat at the store. We ate lots of vegetables. As a child I can remember liking kale and mustard greens and sometimes green poke. Daddy had more of that kind of background than mother did. At Christmas, mother would make . . . four or five kinds of candies and several cakes.

I learned more about farming from my dad than I wanted to! We always had a big garden and grew a tobacco crop. There was always something needing to be done. It was several years after I left home before I would grow a garden. Since we moved to North Carolina I've tried to get back into a little gardening in small areas. I like to do organic gardening and am interested in doing intensive planting—as one crop finishes another is planted in its place. Our food tastes have changed, and we try a lot of different things. In a lot of ways though, our meals are not a lot different from back then; we still eat green beans, mashed potatoes, gravy, fried chicken, and roast beef.

"Is it my turn now?" Phyllis asked as she came in from the kitchen. Phyllis is tall, about five feet nine inches, has a lovely figure, clear creamy skin, dark brown eyes, and black hair. Phyllis has a ready smile, a musical laugh, and a good sense of humor.

I graduated from Berea College with a B.S. degree in home economics and, after I took graduate classes at Eastern State University, I became a registered dietitian. Currently I am employed by the Marriott Corporation as an Administrative Dietitian and also serve some nursing homes in this area as a consultant. I find it very difficult to keep up with nutrition. I sometimes have problems reconciling what I was taught with what I intuitively know about nutrition.

I was born in Oneida, Kentucky. Until I was around four years old, we lived on a farm in Owsley County. My grandparents lived in a house close to us. My older brother and I lived with our parents in a very small house. Later on we moved to Beattyville in Lee County.

That was a big town for us. We had been living about ten miles out in the country up a creek. My great-aunt and uncle lived less than half a mile away, and another great-aunt and uncle lived about a mile from us up a holler.

I remember when electricity was brought in. Boy, was that an event because after all the wiring was done, we had those bare light bulbs! We kept them on a long time that night. Everybody just marveled how in the world that electricity could be brought in and do all of that. The first piece of electrical equipment we got was a washing machine.

Someone said they thought we would have got a refrigerator first of all, but when you think about it, we kept our milk and butter cold in the springhouse. But every week Mother had the chore of washing the clothes. She had a big black pot in which she heated water. She used lye soap and a washboard, and it was an all-day job.

Moving into a town brought quite a change to my life-style. The population was around a thousand. I was the only child except my brother, five years older than me. He did a lot of things that I couldn't do and I felt neglected. I was too small to be bothered with. I can remember asking the adults many questions. I must have really aggravated them because they'd tell me to go play. I remember standing on tiptoe looking into the mirror on the dresser saying, "Now I really want to know the answer to that question. I'm going to remember this so when I get a little older I can ask it again—and they'd better tell me!"

I begged my mother to let me help her cook, and she let me make some cakes, or something I couldn't mess up too badly. I remember when we lived with my grandmother that I did get to wash dishes. She made a special effort that I learn to wash dishes. Of course I had to stand on a stool to do it. Water had to be heated in two pans on the stove and I got to do that. I felt very grown-up.

One of my jobs was to churn. The churn was an old crock with a wooden handle dasher. They bragged on me and made me feel important that I could do the churning.

My grandmothers were both good cooks, as was my mother. We ate simple foods. There was one thing that I can taste right now. I don't have the recipe for it—wish I did. It was a lemon molasses cake. It was like a cupcake. It was baked in a muffin tin. She used molasses and I just really loved those little cakes.

My father and grandfather worked on the farm, and they always needed a good hot breakfast. We would have fried chicken, biscuits, fried potatoes, eggs, and honey.

When we moved to town my father got a job in the oil fields, and he worked there for quite some time. After that, I don't remember the year, he got a job as a janitor in the grade school which was real close to us. He just had to walk down the hill. About the same time I started to school, my mother became a cook in the school. We all went to the same place and my mother got to come home with me which was important because there wasn't anybody to take care of children after school.

When I was nine, we got our first car. It was a '51 Chevrolet. It was black, and boy was it ever a pride and joy. I mean that car was washed and shined and everything. Mother would cook in the mornings as we were getting ready to go to church, and after church we would go and find us a spot, maybe out in the woods, and have our picnic. It was not the typical kind of picnic with fried chicken and potatoes, salad and things like that. But I remember she really liked to do a pot roast and just leave it in the kettle and put it in a box with newspapers around it so that it was still warm. She would have corn bread and slaw, and there was banana pudding for dessert.

One time I made my mother very angry. There's an unwritten law of mountain people that you don't ask them what they had for breakfast, and you don't ask them how much money they make. Well, when I was in grade school I didn't like to eat breakfast very much. My excuse was we had the same old thing all the time. I remember I was at a neighbor's house with Mother one day. Mother was fretting to her friend about how I wouldn't eat breakfast. I said, "If there was ever anything different I might eat breakfast. Who wants biscuits and gravy and eggs and sausage and homemade jam every day?" My mother's face turned white; she was very angry with me.

I remember sometimes as a special treat we would have light bread toasted in the oven. You'd fold it over and make a sandwich. I can't remember the name of that particular bread, but it was in a red wrapper and had some red writing on it. It was a short loaf, but thick like a double-slice of bread. The biggest treat of all was when we visited Grandmother and she would fry bologna and have light bread, toasted in the wood stove, with some gravy. To finish off there would be cantaloupe.

When I got married I tried to be a little more adventuresome in my cooking than my mother had. She did not own a cookbook and thought that it was an insult to even suggest that she needed one. I discovered that wasn't really an unusual attitude to have because when my brother got married I got him and his wife a cookbook. It was *The Joy of Cooking*. When his wife unwrapped the package her face showed total disappointment. I realized then that I had insulted her. She was known to be a good cook.

You see, there was a pride in being able to cook well but it was still the simple things—no combination dishes—just simple things. To this day my mother does not have a cookbook, other than *The Joy of Cooking*, which I got her, and your own cookbook, Sidney, *More Than Moonshine*. Not long ago when I visited my mother she asked me to make a chocolate pie. I said, "Mother, I don't have my recipe and it's been awhile, I don't remember just what all the ingredients are." She looked at me with utter disgust. She must have thought what a waste it was sending me to college where I majored in home economics and I didn't know how to make a chocolate pie without a recipe. Being embarrassed for not living up to her expectations, I did manage to put a chocolate pie together.

I want to say one thing in this interview, and that is that most people in Appalachia grew up eating pinto beans, corn bread, and greens and things like that. You probably used to be as ashamed as I was because those kinds of foods equated with poverty to the outside world. But I look back now as a nutritionist or dietitian, and know that we ate very well because when you combine pinto beans and corn bread you have a complete protein, and you don't really need meat. Also there's lots of fiber there, and when you add coleslaw to that you've got vegetables. That was a balanced diet. Mountain people were rather healthy, and I think it was because of eating things like that—even though they did eat a lot of pork. I think that diet is not the biggest reason for high cholesterol levels. I believe other things enter into it—and one is exercise. But the biggest cause of high levels of cholesterol is stress.

You need a certain amount of stress though to stimulate you to do things. So there's a middle road. I believe in moderation in all things.

LARRY'S CINNAMON TOAST

Butter
Brown sugar
Ground cinnamon, to taste
Bread

Cream butter, brown sugar, and cinnamon together, making a thick paste. Spread the mixture on each piece of bread, making sure to cover entire surface. Place under the broiler and toast until the sugar and butter melt. Let cool before eating. The sugar fuses on the top and forms a sweet crust.

MOTHER'S BLACKBERRY JAM

Fresh blackberries
Sugar

Wash and drain blackberries. Grind. Mix 4 parts blackberries with 3 parts sugar. Cook until thick. Test by placing a spoonful of jam on a saucer and letting it cool.

GRANDMOTHER'S FRUITCAKE

4 cups all-purpose flour
1½ cups brown sugar
½ cup molasses
1 teaspoon baking soda
1 cup buttermilk
1½ cups butter, melted
2 teaspoons baking powder
1 teaspoon ground nutmeg
1 teaspoon ground cinnamon
1 teaspoon ground allspice
1 teaspoon ground cloves
½ pound candied cherries
½ pound candied pineapple
4 ounces citron
1 box dates, chopped
1 box raisins
6 eggs
2 cups nuts

Mix fruit and nuts with flour and brown sugar. Add spices, baking powder, and soda. Add eggs and liquids. Stir until well mixed. Pour into greased cake pan or loaf pan. Bake at 250 degrees for 3½ hours or until wooden pick inserted in center comes out almost clean.

CHOCOLATE BROWNIES

1 cup cocoa
1 cup margarine or butter
2 cups sugar
3 eggs, lightly beaten
1 teaspoon vanilla
1 cup all-purpose flour
1 cup chopped nuts (optional)

Melt butter, add cocoa and sugar and stir until completely mixed. Stir in eggs
and vanilla. Mix in flour until well blended. Add nuts. Pour into greased pan.
Bake at 350 degrees for 35 to 40 minutes or until wooden pick inserted in
center comes out almost clean. Cool in pan on wire rack; cut into squares.

I took an ordinary recipe for zucchini bread and decided to make
it more southern in taste by substituting honey for sugar and whole
wheat for white flour. It produces a moist cakelike loaf and is especially good right out of the oven.

PHYLLIS'S ZUCCHINI BREAD

1 cup vegetable oil
2 eggs, slightly beaten
2 cups honey
2 cups grated raw zucchini
2 teaspoons vanilla
3 cups whole wheat flour
1 teaspoon soda
¼ teaspoon baking powder
1 teaspoon salt
3 teaspoons cinnamon
1 cup walnuts or pecans

Combine eggs, sugar, zucchini, and vanilla. Blend well. Sift in flour, soda,
baking powder, salt, and cinnamon. Do not beat. Stir in walnuts or pecans.
Spoon batter into 2 greased and floured 8½ x 4½ x 2⅛-inch loaf pans. Bake
at 325 degrees for 90 minutes.

The following recipe was one of those newfangled recipes I learned how to make in college. It took a time or two for my father to say that he liked it. I usually made double the recipe since the whole family came to love it. It was great as a leftover served on toast. As is usual with me, I adapted the original recipe to my own taste.

BEEF STROGANOFF

3 tablespoons flour
1 teaspoon salt
¼ teaspoon pepper
1 pound eye-of-round beef
1 cut clove garlic
¼ cup margarine
½ cup chopped onion
1 can undiluted condensed cream of chicken soup
1 pound sliced mushrooms
1 cup sour cream

Rub both sides of meat with garlic. Combine flour, salt, and pepper. Sprinkle flour mixture on meat. With rim of saucer, pound mixture into both sides of meat. The pounding tenderizes meat, and the flour helps meat to brown. Cut meat into 1½ x 1-inch strips. Brown meat strips in deep skillet in margarine, turning often. Add onions, and sauté until golden. Add water, stir to dissolve brown bits in bottom of skillet. Add soup and mushrooms. Cook uncovered over low heat, stirring occasionally until mixture is thick and meat tender— about 20 minutes. Add sour cream and heat, but do not boil. Serve over rice or noodles. Sprinkle with parsley if desired. Makes 4 to 6 servings.

Elizabeth Roe Glenn
Winston-Salem, North Carolina

I ARRIVED *to visit Elizabeth Roe Glenn one gray afternoon in early November. It was darker than usual for the time of day, and one could feel winter in the cold wind. She invited me into her modern, well-furnished living room. Good smells drifted in from the kitchen as we talked. Elizabeth's husband is a retired pediatrician, working at the Department of Veteran Affairs regional office, and she has been preparing some food for their dinner. They have three adult children: two daughters and one son. Elizabeth works in the health care field in continuing care for the elderly.*

My name is Elizabeth Roe Glenn. I have lived here in Winston-Salem for twenty-eight years. My profession is a hospital dietitian. I graduated from the University of North Carolina in Greensboro, and received my training at the medical college of Virginia. Since then I have spent approximately twelve years in the profession—the rest of the time I spent at home rearing children and enjoying cooking. I grew up in the northwestern part of North Carolina in Ashe County. My husband says he came as far back in as he could by car—then swung in on a grapevine to find me! It is a beautiful spot there, and we go often in the summertime. My ninety-two-year-old father still lives there at the old home place. Ashe County borders Virginia in the north and Tennessee in the west. We were about three miles from Virginia and ten miles from Tennessee.

Any social life we had when I was growing up was church-related activities. We had a small Methodist church and we were very active. We never went to Sunday school or church that my mother didn't invite somebody home for dinner.

My mother-in-law has had Sunday dinner with us for thirty years because she is a widow. Growing up, we always had fried chicken, rice, gravy, and vegetables from the farm. In earlier times it was green peas, green beans, carrots, and beets. In later times we found out about broccoli. It grows well in the mountains and became one of our favorite vegetables. We didn't grow okra, and we didn't have grits. I think people outside the area think that all southern people grew up on grits and okra.

A Saturday night ritual on the farm: Daddy would kill the chicken, and we'd cut it up and salt it down—which we don't do now because we have refrigeration. We had a springhouse and a spring run. . . . We kept milk and butter and other things we wanted to keep cold in the stream of cold water. We'd put the kettle with salted chicken in the stream and it would keep until the next day.

We always had a big breakfast. My mother made great homemade rolls and buns (I'll give you the recipe for the rolls). When my children were small I cooked a big breakfast, too. Now we are more likely to have cereal and juice. On special occasions we have Moravian sugar cake for breakfast. Have you ever been introduced to Moravian sugar cake? It's a North Carolina recipe. It's like a sweet breakfast bread with the top covered with brown sugar, butter, and cinnamon.

Ironically, my mother always talked about how she hated cooking. But she was an absolutely marvelous cook and could make a wonderful dish out of whatever was there. When I was eight years old she let me make my first cake. My grandmother came to visit and said, "What do you mean letting that child in there to mess up your kitchen?" My mother said, "She'll never learn till she does it." And so from the time I was eight I was making all the cakes at home. I enjoyed cooking.

Mother usually served fruit desserts on Sunday. A cherry dessert was one of her very favorite things. Always with fried chicken, turkey, or roast pork, she'd make baked cherries with cherries picked off the trees and canned. She'd mix canned cherries with a little flour, sugar, and just a dash of cinnamon, and put them in a baking dish and dot with butter—and they were so yummy. They weren't too sweet, just a nice side dish with pork or poultry. I get nostalgic about that. I've tried it with canned, tart red cherries, but they do not taste the same. My mother also made a wonderful rhubarb pie.

My family always killed hogs in the late fall of the year, around Thanksgiving and Christmas. The neighborhood shared. If somebody didn't like brains, somebody didn't like pig feet, somebody didn't want this, they'd trade off. We had a delightful English family that lived across the road from us, and they loved pig feet, so Mother would always take "Miss Anna" all our pig feet.

The community where I grew up had a woolen mill (that's how the English people got there, they had the woolen mill). And just down the road was a gristmill which my family owned. Cornmeal, flour, whole-grain products—people brought their grain to be ground at the mill. The mill was powered by water. A creek ran right by and they dammed it up and directed it through the mill race.

The old mill is still standing. It's been out of the family for a long, long time. Frequently when we'd go up in the summertime Dick would say, "Wouldn't it be fun to restore that old mill and make a summer home out of it?" It would cost a fortune to do it, I suppose. It has twelve-foot ceilings and stairways that go from one level to another. I always envisioned it would make a beautiful restaurant. But there's not enough tourist traffic in that area to support it. In 1988 the mill was restored as a home.

Even though my children are all grown and married and I have a grandson (five months old who lives with his parents in Winchester, Kentucky) and a granddaughter (three and a half who lives with her parents in Cary, North Carolina), life moves along about the same. I continue to work full time as clinical dietitian at the Triad United Methodist Home—a continuing care community of four hundred residents, and I stay busy with civic interest and professional organizations.

We enjoy living in Winston-Salem. It has a lot to offer in terms of culture. We enjoy the Winston-Salem symphony, the North Carolina School of the Arts—we enjoy the plays there at the Little Theater. I think you can spend your time being involved in what the city has to offer. Whereas when you live in a small town, you spend so much time just getting from one place to another. Of course, I think wherever you live, you should get involved in projects in the community, good service-related projects that help people and, perhaps, enhance the place where you live.

MOTHER'S WONDERFUL ROLLS

1 package yeast
¼ cup lukewarm water
1 cup milk
3 tablespoons sugar
3 tablespoons shortening
1 teaspoon salt
1 egg
3 to 3½ cups flour

Dissolve yeast in warm water. Scald milk. Add sugar, shortening, and salt. Cool and add to yeast mixture. Beat egg well and add to mixture. Gradually add flour. Turn onto floured surface and knead lightly. Place in greased bowl.

Turn dough over so top will be greased. Cover and let rise until double in bulk (about 1 hour). Turn onto floured surface again; work down and shape into rolls. Place on greased pan and let rise again until double in bulk, 45 minutes to 1 hour. Bake in 400 degree oven for 15 to 18 minutes. Makes about 2½ dozen rolls.

The following two recipes are old-time favorites from a church cookbook I edited in 1968. I would now modify them by using cholesterol-free mayonnaise, nonfat yogurt, and corn oil margarine. They are both wonderful to have in the freezer.

CHICKEN TETRAZZINI

1 (8-oz.) package thin spaghetti
10 to 12 chicken breasts or 5 cups diced chicken
½ to 1 cup slivered almonds
½ cup grated Parmesan cheese

SAUCE

2 cans cream of mushroom soup, undiluted
2 teaspoons Worcestershire sauce
¼ teaspoon nutmeg
1 cup mayonnaise
½ cup sherry
½ cup whipping cream, whipped

Cook spaghetti as directed in salt water. Place in 3-quart shallow casserole. Cook chicken, cut in bite-size pieces and spread over spaghetti. Sprinkle with almonds (toasted almonds in small amount of butter). Mix sauce ingredients together and pour over all. Top with Parmesan cheese. Bake at 350 degrees for 30 minutes. This can be made a day ahead or frozen. Makes 10 to 12 servings.

SEAFOOD NEWBURG FOR A PARTY

1½ pounds frozen shrimp, cooked and diced
1 pound Alaskan king crab, drained and diced
½ cup sherry, if desired
1 tablespoon lemon juice
¼ teaspoon nutmeg
1½ sticks butter
½ cup plus 2 tablespoons flour
1 quart half-and-half cream
1½ teaspoons salt
2 egg yolks, beaten
½ cup heavy cream
1 cup grated sharp cheese

Mix seafood, sherry, lemon juice, and nutmeg. Cover and refrigerate several hours or overnight. Melt butter, blend in flour, and stir in half-and-half cream. Add salt and cook over low heat until thickened, approximately 20 minutes. Combine egg yolks and cream. Add to the sauce with grated cheese. Stir until well blended and cheese is melted. Add marinated seafood and marinade. Heat 10 minutes longer. Serve over toast points or patty shells. May be thinned with milk or additional sherry. Makes 12 servings. Freezes well.

Moravian missionaries, members of a Protestant denomination, arising from a fifteenth-century religious reform movement in Bohemia and Moravia, founded the Valle Crucis Mission Center near Banner Elk, North Carolina, in the early part of this century. The Moravians were good cooks. This adaptation of the recipe is from my friend, Julia Ross, who is a master bread maker.

MORAVIAN SUGAR CAKE

1 cup warm water
1½ packages dry yeast
½ teaspoon sugar
2 tablespoons dry milk powder
2 tablespoons instant potatoes
⅓ cup sugar
½ teaspoon salt
1 cup flour
2 eggs
6 tablespoons margarine, melted
½ cup flour
1¼ cups more flour
⅔ cup brown sugar
1 teaspoon cinnamon
⅓ cup melted butter

Put warm water in a large mixing bowl. Sprinkle yeast and sugar over top of water and stir to mix well. When mixture becomes foamy, add dry milk powder, instant potatoes, sugar, salt, and 1 cup flour. Beat 2 minutes on medium speed. Add eggs, margarine, and ½ cup flour. Beat 2 more minutes on high speed. Stir in rest of flour. Cover and set in warm place to rise until double in bulk, approximately 1 hour. When risen, stir the dough and spread in 15 x 1-inch pan. Let rise again until double. Mix brown sugar and cinnamon and sprinkle over dough. Make indentations with fingers and pour the melted butter over top of sugar mixture. Bake at 400 degrees for 15 to 20 minutes.

Jean Seeman
Winston-Salem, North Carolina

PHYLLIS AND LARRY HENSON *told me about Jean Seeman, one of Larry's colleagues at Wake Forest University, a woman who was a good cook and loved to talk about food. I arrived at her house when fall colors covered the trees. Jean met me at the door with a ready smile. She has a robust laugh and sparkling eyes.*

My name is Jean Seeman. I have a Ph.D. in psychology, I'm a former teacher in the psychology department, and am now academic computing manager in the Computer Center at Wake Forest University.

My number-one dream for a long time was to get a house, and finally I did. There are a lot of things to do around a house that I like—gardening with vegetables and flowers, cutting firewood, building my furniture. I like photography and carpentry work. I made my dining table, my entertainment center, and some smaller items. I like living in this city and will stay here at least until my son gets through college.

I have three sisters, and we are all highly verbal and very social kinds of people. I like to be with people and give parties, including inviting people to lunch and dinner. I always thought my upbringing was fairly basic and outdoors-oriented and have come to think of my view of life as southern. We always ate fairly simple kinds of foods and didn't have a television until I was in fifth grade, so we played a lot of games together and read a lot.

When we were young our parents always took us for a Sunday drive, regardless of the weather. We would gather walnuts and hazelnuts, buy watermelons out of the field, get sand for the sandbox. It would be quiet in the woods and we'd see beaver dams. I used to love to go fishing. There was nothing better than sitting by the bank of a river, watching nature, and occasionally seeing the bobber go down. I remember visiting older relatives out in the country and there would usually be a creek, and we'd fish there as kids.

We all like to garden and all have gardens at our homes. One of my sisters finally moved back to a farm even though she works in this city and her husband is a public school administrator. Two of my sisters have goats, dogs, cats, and horses. I do like living in the city because of the greater number of social, entertainment, learning, and shopping opportunities, but every weekend we go home to my parents' house for dinner. My parents live in a small town where both sets of grandparents lived. My father is in his third career in Madison, North Carolina.

My mother and father did not start out as adults with college degrees, but we children have all been encouraged and eager to learn and get higher degrees. All of us have found ourselves liking to do things with our hands—we all like to sew, cook, and make crafts.

My father was reared in Stokes County in a little community called Egypt—which is now underwater because a man-made lake covered it up. My father comes from a family of fifteen children; he is the thirteenth. His parents were farmers, and then later my grandfather moved to Rockingham County and also ran a general store; he was a magistrate and continued farming.

The other set of grandparents were from two little mountain communities called Woolwine and Buffalo Ridge, just north of Stuart,

Virginia. My grandfather became a carpenter and went to Kimball, West Virginia, to work for a while as a carpenter for the mines. He had three children, then his first wife died. When he was thirty-eight he married my grandmother, who was nineteen at the time. They drove to the preacher's house in a buggy, had no ring, and didn't get out of the buggy. They had six more children, but never did have a car.

For a long time we thought our grandmothers were better cooks than our mother, although they cooked similar foods. Our favorite lunch would be corn bread, turnip greens, and pinto beans (unless you count corn-on-the-cob in season). Then we'd chop up onions and put on the pinto beans, and vinegar on the greens. We always had simple things for desserts, apple pie, chocolate pie, and our very favorite, fried apple pie. We all liked homemade macaroni and cheese so much that one Christmas when Grandmother forgot it, we had to find a store that was open so we could buy some macaroni and waited on dinner until it was cooked.

Every summer and winter we'd go back to where the grandparents lived, and all the aunts and uncles and cousins would come. We'd go to my Grandmother Carter's house, my father's mother, in the summer, and get out the big iron pot and make Brunswick stew.

Brunswick stew is a family favorite. To make the stew, we'd boil the beef and throw in chicken carcasses, and when the meat was done we'd take it off the bones and throw in every vegetable we had on hand. So far as I know, we have never had a recipe, and never used wild game that some people use (rabbit, squirrel, alligator). We stirred the stew with a big wooden paddle. Pepper was added, but not much salt, and no other seasonings. We did this recently on a summer day when the temperature was a hundred degrees, so we took turns stirring. We never used anything for a thickener, though as the meat separated and the water cooked out, it became thicker and thicker. Some people used cornflakes to thicken the stew, but we never did. I have seen a recipe for Kentucky burgoo that looks very much like that for Brunswick stew. I've heard people speak of a Brunswick stew made all of chicken, but to our way of thinking, that's just chicken stew. The final touches for Brunswick stew were to serve it with light bread (white loaf bread) in small paper trays.

I forgot to mention how much we all loved watermelon. The whole family would get together and we'd cut one, sprinkle on salt, and eat it that way, unchilled. And then there was ice cream! That was a whole ritual in itself. We made vanilla in the old ice-cream maker and sometimes we'd add fruit—strawberries, peaches, something seasonal. Toward the end of the turning, the adults would put newspaper over the top of the freezer, and the kids would take turns sitting on the top of it to keep it from turning over as the turning of the handle got more and more difficult. I make ice cream a little differently today; I make a cooked custard first, but I still make it, and vanilla is my favorite.

My maternal grandfather had an ulcer so my grandmother had to cook special things for him. One of his favorite things was to take butter and honey and mix them up on a plate, then spread that on hot biscuits. Grandmother Carter died some time ago at ninety-three. She'd cook stew beef and simple things like that. But when my father was growing up, she'd cook things like pork chops, steaks, and mashed potatoes—for breakfast! They worked so hard they needed a heavy breakfast. By the time my grandmother got older, I'd have to go spend weekends with her. She'd send me to the store to get a can of hominy, and we'd eat that a lot. She boiled her coffee on the top of the stove, adding egg shell to the bottom of the pot to settle the grounds. For breakfast, she'd cook bacon, then fry the eggs and the bread in the bacon grease. She'd spread jelly over the fried bread, then add the eggs and bacon, and fold over the bread and eat the whole mess. That sounds nutritionally horrible, but she did live to be ninety-three!

Over the years we've all changed the way we eat. At the time we left home, my father complained that we didn't really know how to cook, but we'd really done a good bit by then. We were missing some information, however. When I was on my own and went to the grocery store for the first time, I didn't realize there were two kinds of flour. I got self-rising instead of plain, and you can imagine how some of the things I cooked turned out. But as we really got into cooking, we'd find recipes we liked and pass them on to Mother, and she gradually began to do things like cut out the fatback. So her cooking has slimmed down, you might say, but has become a lot broader.

My mother did the main cooking at home except when she was sick; then Father would cook, and iron, and do other domestic chores. And he always cooked breakfast when we went camping. There is nothing to beat the smell of coffee and fried potatoes when you wake up in the outdoors. My father doesn't know how to cook a great variety of things, but he could fend for himself if he had to. When we were sick, my mother always made potato soup—it was a rule.

While food was important to our family, other things were also, such as church homecomings and family reunions. But then, food is the important thing at those occasions too, isn't it? In Rockingham County, North Carolina, where my paternal grandfather was born, there are two log cabins. They are kept up but nobody lives in them—no indoor plumbing or electricity, but there is running water in one. We go there once a year for a family reunion. There are tables loaded with food—hams, squash, biscuits, and things like the all-favorite tomato sandwich. You must make tomato sandwiches ahead of time so they are soggy, and be sure to sprinkle on salt and pepper. When I was a child, and my mother was not watching me, on these occasions I'd eat corn, and maybe green beans with new potatoes, then eat some of every kind of dessert there was, and that's all I'd eat.

My favorite Sunday dinner for a while was baked ham, homemade biscuits, home-canned green beans, and potato salad. Depending on the time of year, there might also be fresh sliced tomatoes, corn-on-the-cob, or other available vegetables. While I was in college, my mother remembered my favorite Sunday dinner, and fixed it every time I came home—and forgot that while they had other meals in between my homecomings, every time I came home I had the same meal.

We still eat at my parents every Sunday. When I cook at home, we usually eat light at lunchtime and have our biggest meal at supper-time. I also can't remember the last time I cooked ham and potato salad. A nice Irish Catholic gave me a wonderful Italian recipe called cannelloni, and it is now one of my mother's favorites. Her recipes have grown from fatback with turnip greens and crackling corn bread to baked sea trout and Yorkshire pudding. She will try things she's never tried before.

Housekeeping is not my big thing—there's hardly anything I like least to do. Cooking is another thing, though, and I have some rules: cook in bulk, make multiple use of things, and save leftovers for soup. The only thing I can now in the summer is soup; I have a recipe for tomato soup that makes fourteen quarts. During the winter, when it is especially cold and/or rainy or snowy, I get out two quarts of tomato soup, and all frozen leftovers, and make stew.

I've always had some kind of garden—even in the tiny spaces in back of an apartment I'd grow a few things. I grow squash and cu-cumbers, tomatoes, green onions—all the basics. Lately I have dis-covered fresh basil—I make pesto sauce, which I never heard of when I was growing up. I now have rabbit-eye blueberries as my frontyard hedge, blackberries, a cherry tree, and red raspberries in the yard. There is also rhubarb and asparagus. I believe that your land should feed you, as well as be decorative.

I want to share some of the older recipes with you, the tried-and-true you might say. The first one is a recipe for fried apple pie. This one has been passed down from one generation to the next. This one is my mother's recipe. Her name is Nancy.

NANCY'S FRIED APPLE PIE

1½ cups dried apples
Water
¾ cup sugar
Cinnamon to taste
Pie pastry
Vegetable oil

Stew dried fruit in water to cover. Toward the end of cooking, add the sugar and cinnamon to taste. Roll the pastry in rounds. Place about 2 tablespoons apple filling to one side of the circle, fold the other side over, then seal edges with a fork. Fry pies in cooking oil until brown.

APPLE DUMPLINGS

Make your favorite pie pastry, and roll in rounds large enough to go around your apples. Core apples, but do not peel. Place apple on pastry round, put sugar and cinnamon in the core hole, and dot with butter. Mold the pastry up around the apple, pinching the top well closed so that filling does not boil out. Place in baking dish.

SYRUP

1 cup sugar
¾ cup water
1 teaspoon lemon juice
½ stick margarine

Make a syrup out of the above ingredients. Pour some of this over the apples and bake at 350 degrees until brown. Baste with syrup as they cook.

APPLE CRUMB PIE

⅔ cup sugar
¼ teaspoon salt
¼ teaspoon cinnamon
¼ teaspoon nutmeg
1¼ teaspoon grated lemon rind
1 tablespoon margarine
6 to 8 green apples, pared and sliced
1 unbaked 9-inch pie shell

Blend all ingredients and arrange in pie shell.

SUGAR CRUMB TOPPING

¾ cup packed brown sugar
¼ cup white sugar
¼ teaspoon nutmeg
¼ teaspoon salt
½ cup margarine

Blend ingredients, stirring with fork until margarine is in small pieces. Spoon topping over apples. Bake at 425 degrees for 10 minutes, then set oven to 350 degrees and bake 35 to 40 minutes more.

YAM BISCUITS

½ cup baked mashed sweet potatoes
2 cups flour
1 tablespoon baking powder
¼ cup margarine
1 teaspoon salt
2 teaspoons sugar
½ cup milk

Sift dry ingredients together in bowl. Mix in shortening and mashed yams with an electric beater at medium speed. When mixture appears light and crumbly, gradually add milk, continuing to mix just until ingredients are evenly dampened—do not beat. Flour a surface and turn contents of bowl out. Knead for 35 to 45 seconds. Roll out to thickness of ¾ inch and cut with biscuit cutter. Place about 1½ inches apart on ungreased heavy baking sheet. Reroll leftover dough and cut more biscuits until all is used. Bake on middle rack of preheated 450 degree oven 12 to 15 minutes or until biscuits are lightly browned on top.

Note: Instead of yams, you can add ½ cup of almost any vegetable cooked and mashed. I have used white potatoes, yellow squash, and zucchini. You could also use carrots.

MRS. BROWN'S APPLESAUCE CAKE

2 eggs
½ cup butter
2½ cups flour
1 cup raisins
1 cup chopped dates
1½ cup chopped nuts
2 cups sugar
1 teaspoon allspice
1 teaspoon cloves
2 small jars maraschino cherries (reserve juice)
3 teaspoons baking soda
1 cup applesauce
3 teaspoons cinnamon
½ teaspoon salt

Cream butter and sugar, add eggs and applesauce. Add flour which has been sifted with spices, soda, and salt. Fold in raisins, dates, and nuts. Add cherries, drained and sliced. Pour into a greased, 10-inch tube pan after lining bottom with brown paper. Bake two hours at 275 degrees. Cool in pan 10 minutes, then turn out. When cooled, pour ¼ cup reserved cherry juice on top. Wrap in foil and keep in a cool place.

Pam Dellen

Indianapolis, Indiana

MY YOUNGEST SISTER, *Sharon Rose Clark, lives in Indianapolis. When she heard I was interviewing people she suggested her sister-in-law Pam Dellen might have an interesting viewpoint for the book. She arranged for us to come to the Dellen home on Saturday morning. It was February, and cold, with a sharp wind blowing. I saw a large house sitting back surrounded by acres of lawn and a pond within sight of the house from the side. The pond was frozen, and some children, supervised by an adult, were testing to see how solid the ice was.*

My name is Pam Dellen and I live in Indianapolis. We named our home Whispering Pines Ranch, which is on about eighteen acres of land. As you can see, there is a pond in which we swim in the summertime and ice-skate in the winter—when it freezes solidly enough.

My husband is also a native of Indianapolis. He is president of the Rock Island Refinery. I was a hairdresser when I met him. As you can imagine his people are very different in every respect from my people who came here from Kentucky before I was born. After Father retired they couldn't wait to go back home to Kentucky.

My life-style today is very fast-paced. That's what I like about going to visit my folks in Kentucky because you can get back in the hills and you can sit back and kick your shoes off, take a deep breath, and relax and enjoy the people that come to visit you. I think, why can't we be like that here in Indianapolis? Things are so hustle-bustle and you just don't take the time to sit back and relax. I don't work outside the home, but I keep very busy here. In the summer I do most of the mowing because of my husband's work schedule.

A typical dinner at my house will be chicken or meat loaf, one vegetable, and a potato of some kind, no bread. No extra starches or sweets.

My father is originally from Frankfort, Kentucky, and my mother from Crittenton County, Kentucky. Mother was born in Florida. I'm not sure how her parents got to Florida. . . . Then they lived in Marion, Kentucky, on Cotton Patch, which was the name of the hill they lived on. My mother had to live with an aunt and an uncle, who were brother and sister, because her parents lived so far back the bus couldn't get in to take her to school. She spent most of her school years living with this aunt and uncle near the bus stop. She was an only child, and her parents had a little more money than some of the people in Marion, so she was able to go to college at Western Kentucky University in Bowling Green. She didn't finish, however, but stopped after she learned some secretarial law and skills. She got a job in Frankfort, where she met my father. Even though my mother didn't get a college degree, she was qualified to do secretarial work, but after she married and had children she never worked outside the home.

They got married and, after several years, Father saw where they had job openings at Greyhound Buslines. They moved to Indianapolis, and he got a job with Greyhound. They bought their own home and that's where we lived. He worked there until his retirement, and then they moved down to mother's home place in Marion, Kentucky, and that's where they are today. They moved because they just had

an ordinary house here with a very small backyard. Father still likes
the outdoors and wanted some breathing room. In fact, they had two
different farms that they had inherited and couldn't see letting either
one sit idle.

My grandmother was an immaculate housekeeper and very busy.
She was forty years old when Mother was born, and she didn't have a
lot of patience with a little one at that time. Mother was real close to
her father and stayed out on the farm with him.

At home when I was a child a typical meal for us would have been
pork chops, mashed potatoes, macaroni and cheese—lots of starchy
things. We didn't eat a lot of meat. We never went hungry, but I
think we were more filled on starchy things like biscuits, gravies, and
cakes. There was always bread on the table at my mother's. Father ate
bread with every meal, and so do my brothers.

Sunday dinners for us were not special in the way they were when
my mother grew up in Kentucky. She didn't really cook that much on
Sunday as she would every night during the week. She always cooked
a lot of food. She would put the leftovers up and have them later. She
could do so much with leftovers. . . . She would use leftover mashed
potatoes to make potato cakes or chicken salad. She'd grind bologna
and make a sandwich spread that was really good. Today I think back
and I don't know how she did it.

Mother baked a lot, seemed like she was always in the kitchen.
The difference between the kinds of food we had with that of the
neighbors, for example, was that Mother always loaded the table with
lots of food. I don't remember the neighbors having as much or as
starchy foods.

I remember a plain yellow cake that Mother used to make on
which she used her own chocolate sauce. I can remember sitting
around the table with our cake waiting for the sauce to finish, and she
would be standing there stirring it. It wasn't fudge, it was more watery

than fudge sauce, but it was just delicious. While it was still warm she'd pour it on the cake and we just inhaled it; it was delicious.

Mother took advantage of some prepared things when they came out, like cake mixes, but she didn't take any shortcuts as far as her meats or vegetables were concerned. But she didn't do anything fancy like we do—green bean casseroles, for example. For one thing, Father wouldn't have eaten a casserole because he wants to see his meat and his vegetables and his potatoes separate on a plate.

Mother's ancestors were German and they put sugar in everything even the vegetables, potato salad, spaghetti sauce, macaroni and cheese. When I go by her recipes I've learned to eliminate some things. I'll confess though that what I fix never tastes as good as when she fixes it. I have been known to cook chili for my husband and children and eliminate the sugar but then make a pot for me with sugar because that's the way it tastes best to me.

My grandfather's name was Martin Luther Clift; my grandmother's name was Martha Ann Hughes. My mother doesn't have too many living relatives left, except as far as the fifth and sixth cousins there are still a lot of them down there.

We went back home to Kentucky every chance we got, generally about once every two or three months. Grandmother didn't have a telephone, so she kept in touch by letters. She was a neat lady, even to the day she died at eighty-six. She was always pretty independent.

On my father's side there were ten children. He had four sisters and one brother left, and they all raised tobacco. I can remember when he was even real young; they pulled him out of school so he could help in the tobacco fields. I don't remember anything about his mother; they were gone before I was here.

QUICK CORN BREAD

2 cups self-rising cornmeal
1 can cream-style corn
1 cup sour cream
½ cup oil

Mix ingredients and bake. A good, consistent recipe.

PORK CHOPS AND CREAM GRAVY

4 ½ to ¾ inch-thick loin pork chops
Salt and pepper to taste
¼ cup hot vegetable oil
2 tablespoons plain flour
1½ cups milk

Season chops with salt and pepper, and brown on both sides in oil. Drain on paper towels, and set aside. Reserve pan drippings.

Add flour to drippings; cook over medium heat until bubbly, stirring constantly. Add milk and cook until thickened, stirring constantly. Season to taste with salt. Add chops to gravy, cover, and simmer 45 minutes. Yields 4 servings.

COUNTRY FRIED STEAK AND CREAM GRAVY

2 to 2½ pounds boneless round steak
1 teaspoon salt
½ teaspoon pepper
½ teaspoon garlic salt
½ cup plain flour
½ cup milk
½ cup vegetable oil
¼ cup plain flour
2 cups milk
½ teaspoon salt
¼ teaspoon pepper

Pound steak to ¼-inch thickness and cut into serving pieces. Sprinkle steaks with 1 teaspoon salt, ½ teaspoon pepper, and garlic salt. Dredge steak in ½ cup flour, and dip in ½ cup milk. Dredge steak in flour again. Brown steaks in hot oil in large skillet. Remove from skillet, and drain on paper towels. Set aside.

Pour off pan drippings, reserving 3 tablespoons. Add ¼ cup flour to drippings; cook over medium heat until bubbly, stirring constantly. Add 2 cups milk; cook until thickened, stirring constantly. Stir in ½ teaspoon salt and ¼ teaspoon pepper. Add steak to gravy and cover. Reduce heat and simmer 25 minutes. Remove cover, and cook an additional 5 minutes. Makes 8 servings.

Jackie Christian
Madison, Tennessee

JACKIE CHRISTIAN *came to campus to work with Berea
College's Country Dancers—a performing group of students directed
by John Ramsay, a faculty member. I had heard she was a gourmet
cook as well as a good dancer. She agreed to meet me at John's house
the next day and tell me about her work.*

*Jackie greeted me at the door and invited me into John's kitchen. The
sun shone through the windows, and a tea kettle simmered on the stove. We
sat at the kitchen table. Jackie had curly blond hair, fair skin, and a
beautiful smile. Not very tall, her slim body seemed to be packed with
energy. She had on a vintage dress and soft black buttoned shoes. I asked if
she collected vintage clothing.*

I have always worn vintage laces, Victorian dresses, even when I was
a little girl. I've always been intrigued with the old crocheted
pieces. . . . At Christmas, my aunts would give me crochet instead
of toys and things. My mother made me collars. It is sort of stylish
now to dress in old-fashioned clothes, but I collected when other
people thought it was eccentric.

I guess I have always been sort of different, sometimes ahead of
my age. For example, I always knew that being older was more
important than being younger. There are two kinds of women when
they get older: the crotchety, old, negative, neurotic woman, and the

wonderful older lady who is gracious and full of life. I always wanted to be one of the latter kind. I thought maybe that I would be wise if I was older. When I was a teenager and in my early twenties, all the girls were getting suntans, but I didn't. I knew it could ruin my skin.

I was born in 1945. I guess I led an unusually independent life even before the revolution of the sixties became so widespread. I give the credit to my parents and grandmother for the best qualities I possess. I grew up in Northford, Alabama, which is a suburb of Tuscaloosa. My family came from the foothills of the southern Appalachian Mountains, from farms and the mining area up near Jasper, Alabama. Later they migrated out to Tuscaloosa. My family lived with my paternal grandmother until I was in the third grade.

My Grandmother was a very good influence in my life. She grew flowers and vegetables. Every Saturday morning she and I would take them to the curb market. I remember we'd shell peas and beans and stuff and we'd seal them in little packets. It was fun. There were always people there who played dominoes. Somebody would come by with a fiddle and there'd be music and dancing.

My family gave me an awful lot of opportunities. They believed in education. If you go and get a college degree, they would say, your son can get his and go on and become a doctor. They worked hard so that I could have these advantages. Dad did coaching all day and then drove a city transit bus until about midnight. My mother always grew a garden and canned and froze vegetables and fruit. They both taught me to work—I even picked cotton one time. I had cousins who lived in the country and I got to spend part of every summer with them. I learned to milk cows and other country chores. Basically though, I grew up on the fringe of the city.

Dad was the coach at the local high school (this was during World War II). He introduced square dancing in physical education classes. My mother and father courted while going to community dances. My mother does some of the steps—one very close to a black bucking step. My father would turn on the radio in the den and teach me to slow dance. I thought it was the greatest thing in the world.

I took dance classes as a child. I started in classes for tap and ballet when I was three years old. I spent most of my youth in dance classes and studying the piano. I dreamed of being a professional dancer some day.

I married while still in high school, had a son, and then my marriage ended. I had dreamed of being a professional dancer, but marriage and a child put an end to that.

Dad still grows corn and some of it is ground into cornmeal. He grew sorghum cane when my son was small. Father took him to the cane mill where they were having a stir-off and he came back looking like a tar baby. He had the experience of seeing how a stir-off was done. That's one more generation that can look back and say, "I didn't do it much but I remember how it was done." Dad always told my son a lot of stories—not fairy tales but goat stories! You see Dad had goats when he was growing up.

You know, you hear a lot of talk nowadays about people passing down their songs and ballads and the old ways of doing things, but you don't hear much about the old dances being handed down from generation to generation. That's the way it got started, however.

After my son had been in college for a year I felt he would be OK. I was in Birmingham; he was in Tuscaloosa, and he was happy in school. I had raised him by myself from the time he was five years old. I knew that now [that] he was in college, he would probably never be with me for any length of time again. It was not important for me to be in any particular place. It was time for me again. I found that your dreams never leave you, you just have to find them again.

I had lived in Birmingham for nine years then moved to Nashville, Tennessee. I had worked in marketing and advertising for about twenty years—supporting myself and my son.

I had done folk and square dancing as well as ballroom and ballet. In Tennessee I heard about buck dancing and was fascinated. Buck dance is an American folk dance, as is clogging; both sort of come under one umbrella. But it's really two separate dances, and they both have pretty much separate histories.

Clogging primarily came to America from the European dance customs—something like the Irish jig, Lancaster clog, and Welsh clog. The buck dance goes back to its roots in Africa where the natives were dancing flat-footed on the ground, doing ceremonial dances, using a lot of body movement. When the slaves brought it to America they had to blend because they were not allowed to use their drums and so forth. They would see white people doing English dances and quadrilles. So they used the form and added their own flat-foot buck, and the old buck-and-weave. They adapted banjo music to the English music. Buck dance is the basis of tap dance in America. It just differs from clogging in the body movement.

A friend said to me, "Look, if you like buck dancing, why don't you go see Robert Spicer. He's an old mountain man who has preserved buck dancing, and teaches it." I got his telephone number and called. He said, "Well, you can call me back in two weeks." I called back and he said, "Call me back in two weeks and we'll try to set up a time, see what you can do." When I called for the third time he said, "You can come on Tuesday, we'll see what kind of dancer you are." He's had so many people in his life that you have to show him you are really interested before you get to see him. He moves his locale to suit his vocation. He said he'd meet me at Granny's Restaurant.

I took a friend with me because she said I didn't need to be in the backwoods of Tennessee alone at night. She drove her car which happened to be a pink Thunderbird. I had on a Christian Dior warmup suit, and she had on Norma Kali. We drove up a gravel driveway and pickup trucks were parked outside Granny's Restaurant. She looked at me real wide-eyed, being the city girl that she is, and

said, "I think I'll take off my leg warmers." In all my pseudosophisti-
cation, I was really out of place inside that restaurant. That has all
come off since I have spent so much time with Mr. Spicer in that
area.

I did something like an informal apprenticeship with Mr. Spicer; I
had to pass every test. He said, "Well kid, I'm not gonna tell it all to
you at once." He is a wise old fox and knows how to keep a student
hanging on. He said, "The first thing I've got to teach you is about
people, if you are gonna teach dancing you got to teach people." Mr.
Spicer doesn't dance anymore, but he has this progression of dancers
that he's trained or worked with.

I took lessons from him for almost a year. Twice a week . . . I
drove from Nashville to Dixon, Tennessee. There was no actual
dance structure. I asked him a lot of questions. He'd say, "You're
missing a beat; it's like rhythm buck dance. It's the black buck
dance." I'd ask where I missed a beat? He'd say, "You're just missing
one; put it in there." I'd try to do what he said. "Naw, put it before
that other one," he'd say. It was a trial-and-error type of learning.
The more I learned the more I knew I didn't know, and I wanted to
know why.

I don't know when it happened, but suddenly buck dancing became a career, a cause, a vocation. I have never found anything that
satisfied me so well. It was like all of a sudden I had slipped on a glove
that fit perfectly.

My friends scoffed, "You can't do anything with buck dancing!"
But I've always been stubborn when told I couldn't do something. I
believed that if you worked really hard, and that's what you really
wanted to do, you could do it. There is no obstacle that you cannot
get over or around if that's what you want to do. Robert Spicer said,
"If you want to do it, you can. Just figure it out." I worked very hard
and figured it out.

Since I started performing I have seen changes come about, influences that affected the people even in Dixon. Then people added this new stuff—they're doing clogging now to disco music! There's nothing wrong with that as long as you know where you came from. Well, I saw these influences beginning to affect the buck dance, and I got real concerned, because once it's gone it will be hard to get it back. We will probably never ever have it back.

Dance is an unusual art: it's passed on in the folk tradition by observation and survival depends on seeing. Mr. Spicer is a survivalist; he's kept the dance intact in Dixon. What I'm doing is like a revival. Obviously I don't live there, I am not part of that folk way, but I'm the revival person in the chain to keep it alive. I had to decide what to do with buck dancing. I began teaching in Nashville. I put the steps on paper, one of the first times it's ever been done, though I'm sure people have done it other ways. I sort of condensed buck dance until I got to the very foundation. Then I developed a teaching method, a structured way to go.

I teach people basic dance skills and techniques, get their body movements going, and start building from that. I taught buck dance to tap dance teachers at the Southern Association of Dance Masters so they could go back and teach it in the dance schools. So I have made buck dancing a total career. People wonder how I make a living doing that. I say, "Well, my standard of living has come down a little bit, but my level of happiness has risen."

But you wanted to talk about cooking. I love to cook; that's the only domestic talent that I have. I have around a thousand cookbooks! I like regional cookbooks, those put out by clubs, churches, etc. Those are all someone's very special recipes. I have to confess that I seldom follow a recipe exactly. I'll get a recipe out for basics, perhaps, but adapt the recipe.

I read somewhere that Wallis Simpson's favorite breakfast was a rasher of bacon sprinkled with brown sugar. I thought that was neat and tried it right away. I sprinkled brown sugar on some bacon and cooked it. It was wonderful. I find little cooking tips in all kind of places. I took Chinese cooking courses when I was in Birmingham, and do a lot of Chinese cooking. We didn't eat meat very much when I was a child. Our lunch was always vegetables. We might eat meat in the evenings. My grandmother raised chickens; Dad used to go squirrel hunting and we had squirrel. When I was small I used to eat brains. The cooks would scramble the brains and eggs together. When I got older I decided I didn't like brains.

My grandmother was one of the strongest women you'll ever meet. She was the matriarch of the family, totally. She was a wonderful cook. She used to fry potatoes in the oven—she'd cut the potatoes real thin, matchstick pieces. She'd put these into a pan to which she'd added some grease. These she would cook in the oven, turning the pan every now and then.

I remember my grandmother's chicken and dumplings. I tried and tried for years to make chicken and dumplings like she did. Then I adapted my own method, different from anyone else I know. One friend said my way is like having dumplings and chicken gravy.

Now that I live alone I don't do as much cooking as I did when my son was home. Because I had to work full time, I had to plan ahead and use leftovers. You can do wonders with leftovers! I love to bake breads.

I've always loved vegetables. I can go a few days with meat and sandwiches but then I have to have a vegetable meal. The only night I have free in my schedule now is Monday night. That is when I have to entertain people. I try to have people over once a month. I have always had a real sense of home; wherever I am, I create home around me.

Many people have been good to me; they're like my family, my extended family. We are all busy; we stay on the road. So before Christmas I start trying to get everyone together once a month. We do this Monday night thing once a month now. I cook for the whole crowd. Whoever's in town comes. I had chicken and dumplings last time we got together. I had to make two Dutch ovens full of it, about eight quarts for the people who were there. A crisp green salad and sweet pickles complete the meal. I have made broccoli-and-corn casserole, candied sweet potatoes, English peas and mushrooms, cole-slaw, and a vegetable tray to serve at these suppers. I make quick lemon pies.

I cook a lot of natural foods. I also use honey a lot instead of sugar. As much as I am now dancing, I am now having to adjust my diet because I need more protein and ready energy from carbohydrates.

I eat sweet potatoes more now because they are better for you. They have more nutrients and minerals than white potatoes. I eat salads through the day and I also eat lots of fruit.

You know, I like to give food as gifts. This Christmas, instead of baking so much, I went to Alabama and bought unprocessed pecans. So many of the people I know are into natural food diets—especially in the music business—I didn't want to make cookies or anything like that. So I gave pecans as Christmas presents. When I went to Christmas parties I sandwiched pecans with cream cheese and honey. I made pumpkin bread and took that along also.

I also make breads. I have one of those pans where you can actually make four loaves of bread at one time (I have to cut corners where I can.) Usually I make basic whole wheat bread or rolls. It's therapy for me to get in the kitchen. Nothing in the world smells better than bread baking.

On my birthday this year I invited friends over and I cooked for them. Some of them thought I shouldn't have to cook because it was my birthday. But that was my way of giving back to them for the friendship and love they had shared with me. I don't think of that as drudgery—to get in the kitchen and really cook.

CHICKEN AND DUMPLINGS

1 whole chicken with giblets
Sherry
1 teaspoon lemon peel
2 tablespoons fresh parsley, chopped
Dash of salt and pepper
2 cups self-rising flour
1 to 2 hard-boiled eggs

Stew chicken in sherry, lemon peel, parsley, salt, and pepper. Remove from heat, cool, and take chicken from bones.

Add butter to broth and heat to boiling. Put 2 cups self-rising flour in bowl. Add broth to flour, and mix until stiff enough to roll out. Roll out thin and cut into small strips.

Put strips back into broth and cook. Add 1 or 2 chopped boiled eggs to broth and dumplings.

Boil giblets separately then chop and add to dumplings. Stir. Serve hot.

QUICK LEMON PIE

1 graham cracker crust
1 can condensed milk
½ cup lemon juice
1 (8 oz.) package cream cheese
3 egg yolks
1 teaspoon lemon peel

Mix ingredients and put in crust. Chill until very cold. Tastes like a cross between cheesecake and lemon meringue pie.

Glen and Marsha Van Winkle

Renfro Valley, Kentucky

I INTERVIEWED *Glen and Marsha Van Winkle one sunny day in October when the brisk air smelled like wine and multicolored leaves drifted to the ground. I parked the car beside their garage as instructed and followed the path along the side and back until I came to a small gate. I could hear water trickling and saw a little fountain as I entered into the small courtyard. Pots of ferns and other green plants were hung on hooks in the walls. I stepped up two steps to the front door of their house and rang the bell. I kept looking back at the waterfall, the collected native stones sitting around, the beautiful plants.*

Glen and Marsha are a married couple, in their early forties, each with his and her own career, but together they create beautiful stained-glass objects. Making the stained glass has turned into a consuming but profitable hobby for them. Glen is lanky and tall, with light brown hair, and a friendly smile. Marsha suggested that I talk to Glen first.

My Father was born in Rockcastle County, and my Mother was born in Pulaski County. She met my father while he was in the Civilian Conservation Corps. I was born in Berea, Kentucky, at the Berea College Hospital, on April 30, 1950. My parents' names are Aster and Jane Van Winkle. I have one brother, younger than me, and two older sisters. I attended grade school at Disputanta and at Round Stone Elementary School. I graduated from Mt. Vernon High School, and attended Berea College, where I got a B.A. in education. I did graduate work at Eastern Kentucky University.

I went into teaching because I believed I had something to contribute. I was the principal at Round Stone School for three years; prior to that I taught there ten years. I am currently working with the dropout program in the Rockcastle County school system.

When I was a child Mother did most of the cooking. Every once in a while Dad would scramble eggs, fry potatoes, something like that he wanted to eat. My sisters also helped cook, and the chore that was assigned to me was to set the table. I didn't have too much of an interest in cooking at that time. The two things I best remember that Mother cooked were her fried chicken and dried apple pies.

Our breakfasts were always big. We had biscuits, gravy, and some type of meat. Anything from ham, sausage, bacon, eggs, and sometimes oatmeal. On special occasions or on Sunday we would have pancakes and syrup. She would caramelize the sugar on top of the stove, add water, and serve as syrup. I think breakfast is the most important meal of the day.

When I was very young my father farmed for a living. He had a fifty-acre farm and grew standard crops of corn, tobacco, hay, and kept some livestock. Then when I was maybe in fifth grade, he started doing construction work. You see he had learned how at the 3-C Camp—Civilian Conservation Corps—which was a New Deal project. He was born in 1912 and grew up during the depression years. He was in the project, and then in the army during World War II. He did construction for a while then was hired by the Rockcastle County government to be a road grader operator. He worked many years until he got so sick he had to stop. He did not live long after he had to give up his job.

Marsha is very pretty with fair skin and blond hair. While she has a tendency to plumpness, she dresses so tastefully that one is not aware of her size. She is very quiet, never makes small talk, but one listens to every word she does say. There is a restfulness, a tranquility, about her presence.

I was born in the Fort Logan Hospital in Stanford, Kentucky, because at that time there was no hospital in Rockcastle County, where my parents lived. Their names were Samuel D. Whitaker and Ona Hysinger Whitaker. I attended . . . Mt. Vernon Elementary and High School. Then I later went to Berea where I received a B.A. with a major in both agriculture and biology.

As fate would have it though, I could not find a job in my field in Rockcastle County. You see up to my time no woman had ever applied and it was strictly a male-dominated work area. So I got a job with the Kentucky Human Resources Department. I worked as a social services worker for around six years. Then I was transferred to a position of training officer where I traveled throughout the state. Currently I am field service supervisor for the Laurel County office.

When I was a child, during Dad's vacation from work and often just on weekends, we used to travel to Lake Cumberland and camp out. My mother is a very outdoor-oriented person. Perhaps that's why I ended up liking to cook and subsequently doing a lot of it inside. As a child, I remember breakfasts were big meals. We had biscuits, meat, eggs, and gravy. On Sundays, I remember, quite often we had fried chicken for breakfast.

My father worked for the Kentucky Stone Company far twenty-two years. He was a drill helper. As a result of his job, he breathed a lot of rock dust which resulted in emphysema.

I always made good grades in school, better than my sister and brother. Not that I received any more encouragement than they, but even from that young of an age my parents, grandparents, and other relatives all automatically assumed that I would go to college. After high school it seemed the natural next step to enroll in Berea College. My family and people in the community have had a long association with the college. In fact, Glen and I just discovered the other day that my great-grandfather, Harry Chasteen, was one of the very first persons from Rockcastle County ever to attend Berea College.

My grandmother was a very good cook, and I was lucky enough to get part of her collection of recipes, many of which are just handwritten. She also had a number of pamphlet-type cookbooks, the kind you send in labels for. She raised my mother and her younger brother. I have just limited recollections of my father's parents. Both of them died when I was four or five years old. My father was quite a bit older than my mother. My roots run deep in Rockcastle County.

I enjoy cooking. I especially enjoy it if it's for a small dinner party for friends. I have a large collection of cookbooks.

Glen adds: Marsha is one of the best cooks I know. She cooks better than my mother and grandmother did—perhaps because they just cooked traditional foods and Marsha tries new recipes. Whatever it is she beats them by a mile.

I follow a recipe exactly if it's the first time. After that I make variations. One of my recipes that you like, Sidney, is Chicken Tarragon. I found the basic recipe years ago in some magazine or other. I probably used most of the ingredients that I use now. Apparently I discarded the magazine and since that time have adapted it to the point where I'm not sure it remotely resembles what it was the first time.

CHICKEN TARRAGON

Boneless chicken breasts, pounded to ¼-inch thick.
Fresh mushrooms
2 tablespoons half-and-half cream
1 tablespoon butter or cooking oil
Dash of salt and pepper

MARINATE

1 egg white, slightly beaten with fork
2 tablespoons gin or vodka

Marinate chicken 1 to 2 hours before cooking. Take out and brown in butter—cooks quickly. Sauté mushrooms in drippings until almost done. Add salt and pepper to cream to make sauce. Put a little tarragon in sauce at first and gradually add to your taste. Pour over chicken pieces and serve hot.

Recipes from My Friends

Sandy Chowning, *Berea, Kentucky*

My husband and I were invited to a brunch at Sandy Chowning's home. When we arrived, the house was filled with the wonderful aroma of something baking in the oven. There was a platter of fresh fruit in the center of the table. When the guests were seated, Sandy poured coffee, served pieces of warm sausage quiche and fruit. Everything was very good, especially the quiche. I asked Sandy for the recipe which she graciously copied for me.

I do not remember where I got the recipe but I have had it a long time. A great side dish to serve with this is half of a grapefruit sprinkled with brown sugar and cinnamon and topped with a cherry. Also, one small can of crab may be substituted for sausage, leave off the mushrooms.

SAUSAGE AND MUSHROOM QUICHE

9-inch deep dish pastry shell
1 jar or can sliced mushrooms
1 pound sausage (I use mild)
1 tablespoon parsley
2 eggs
1 cup evaporated milk
½ cup Parmesan cheese
¼ teaspoon salt (optional)

214

Crumble sausage in skillet and cook until brown. Drain excess grease. In a bowl, beat eggs, evaporated milk, and cheese. Blend in sausage, mushrooms, and salt. Pour mixture into pastry shell. Bake at 400 degrees for 25 to 30 minutes, or until well browned and set. Let cool for 10 minutes before serving.

Ruth Davis, *Berea, Kentucky*

I have known Ruth Davis for over two decades, first as a neighbor across the street, then as landlady when we rented a house next door to her. A retired school teacher and administrator, Ruth is a lover of good books and good food, although she has to be careful what she eats because she is a diabetic. The following recipes are old ones that her mother made when Ruth was a child.

FRUIT LOAF

1 pound chopped dates
4 slices chopped candied pineapple
¼ pound chopped candied cherries
1 cup pecan bits
1 can coconut
1 can condensed milk

Grease a small loaf pan and line with two layers of wax paper. Bake at 350 degrees for 1 hour. Leave in oven 15 minutes after it is baked. Cool and wrap in wax paper. Store in refrigerator. Serve only very thin slices because it is very rich.

On my mother's side we had Aunt Mary Neal. She and her husband owned and ran the River Inn on the Ohio River. Her husband tended the channel light at night. I remember seeing him working around it in early evenings when we would visit Aunt Mary. Two of the following recipes are her's and became favorites in our home. The Graham Cracker Loaf became a traditional Christmas treat, and a regular at Mother's Ladies Aid meetings. She always cut up dates (and it's better that way), but I confess sometimes I use date bits instead of going to the trouble of cutting the dates into little bits.

GRAHAM CRACKER LOAF

1 pound graham crackers, rolled fine
1 pound small marshmallows
1 pound chopped dates
1 cup chopped nuts
1 cup thick cream

Save ½ cup of cracker crumbs to roll loaf in. Mix other ingredients and form into a loaf. Roll in crumbs. You may roll loaf in damp cloth. Keep chilled. Slice and serve with whipped cream.

My oldest brother was a good cook and always collected recipes. One year a woman whom everyone called Aunt Ruth won first place at the Madison County Fair with the following recipe. Afterward my brother asked her for the recipe. She sent it to him. As soon as he read the ingredients he knew she had left something out (he found out later that she had because she really didn't want anyone else to bake her cake), but when he talked with her again she added what had been omitted.

AUNT RUTH'S RED DEVIL FOOD CAKE

2 cups buttermilk
2 teaspoons soda
1 cup shortening
3 cups sugar, sifted twice
3 tablespoons cocoa
3 eggs
3 cups cake flour, sifted three times
Red food coloring

Add soda to buttermilk; stir and set aside. Cream shortening and sugar, then beat in eggs one at a time. Add buttermilk alternately with flour and cocoa, sifted together. Beat well and pour into 3 round greased and floured pans. Bake at 325 degrees for 35 minutes. Cream powdered sugar and butter together, add red food coloring. Frost between each layer as you stack them, and then frost top and sides of cake.

Grover V. Farr, Berea, Kentucky

Grover and I were married in January 1970, and moved, with my six-year-old son, Bruce Alan, from Berea to Asheville, North Carolina, where I enjoyed getting acquainted with my husband's large family in Asheville, Black Mountain, and Swannanoa. They entertained us at receptions, dinners, and parties. We invited a few of them at a time for lunch and dinner at our small apartment in the Asheville Arms. We both were good cooks, collected recipes, and delighted in finding a good new recipe as well as adapting an old recipe into a favorite new one. Later on, we came back to live in Berea and enjoyed planning small dinner parties for old and new friends. One of our favorite meat dishes for company was pot roast with sour cream.

POT ROAST WITH SOUR CREAM TOPPING

1 tablespoon butter
1 (3 to 4 lb.) beef pot roast (round or blade bone)
1 teaspoon salt
¼ teaspoon pepper
½ teaspoon monosodium glutamate (MSG)
1 (10½ oz.) can condensed cream of celery soup
½ cup raw onion rings
1 cup sour cream at room temperature
1 teaspoon horseradish

Preheat a covered baking dish or oven-proof skillet to 325 degrees.

Melt butter in a large skillet and brown meat slowly. Place in baking dish; sprinkle meat with salt, pepper, and MSG. Spread soup over top and add onions. Cover and bake 2½ hours or until meat is tender. Remove from oven.

Pour off 2 cups drippings and set aside for gravy. Gently blend horseradish into sour cream. Spread mixture on top of roast; return to oven, uncovered for 3 to 5 minutes to glaze sour cream.

GRAVY

2 cups drippings
¼ cup water
2 tablespoons all-purpose flour

Gradually add ¼ cup water or milk to 2 tablespoons flour to make smooth paste. In saucepan heat drippings to boiling. Remove from heat and gradually add flour mixture, stirring constantly. Return to heat and cook, stirring constantly, until of thickened consistency.

Grover loves meat loaf and was always looking for new and different ways to make it. He experimented with various recipes until he came up with this one which became his favorite.

GROVER'S MEAT LOAF

3 pounds ground beef
2 cups bread crumbs
½ cup Heinz 57 Sauce
¼ teaspoon salt
1 pound pork sausage
⅔ cup tomato ketchup
⅛ cup Worcestershire sauce
½ teaspoon black pepper

Mix all ingredients together and place in loaf pans.

SAUCE

6 tablespoons sugar
6 tablespoons white vinegar
4 tablespoons cooking sherry
6 tablespoons water

Pour over meat loaf and place in oven. Bake at 300 degrees for 1 hour or until done. Makes 2 loaves.

Carol Ferguson, *Sonora, Kentucky*

Carol and her husband John Ferguson have their own independent trucking business. Known as a truck-driving storyteller, John is on the road much of the time. When he is not driving, he'll be somewhere telling stories. Carol does the bookkeeping for their business, is active in the Baptist church, sews for herself and her two daughters, edits a newsletter, and takes care of her mother. An excellent cook, Carol's cinnamon rolls are something to dream about. I asked her for some of her best recipes, and she chose some old favorites of her mother's to share in this book.

When my Father was in the last stages of cancer, he kept talking about a cake his mother made that was very good. He said the cakes Mother and I made didn't have the old-fashioned flavor like the ones he remembered as a boy. From all he said about it, I thought it must be the 1-2-3-4 cake, I'd heard about. I started to hunt for the recipe. I found a recipe in a magazine and made it for him. He said it tasted more like the one his mother used to make, than anything else he'd had. I still wasn't satisfied with the results, so I kept on searching. I wrote to a magazine that listed requests for recipes. I received about twenty replies. I worked with them and made my own recipe from the different ideas that I received. I believe the secret is the extra vanilla. The beaten egg whites make it more moist, I think.

OLD-TIME CAKE

1 cup butter
2 cups sugar
3 cups plain flour
4 eggs
1 cup milk
2 teaspoons vanilla
3 teaspoons baking powder
4 teaspoons cornstarch

Cream butter and sugar. Separate eggs and add yolks one at a time to creamed mixture. Save whites for beating. Sift flour, baking powder, and cornstarch together. Combine milk and vanilla. Add the dry ingredients and milk alternately to creamed mixture and beat well. Beat egg whites until they form stiff peaks. Gently fold them into mixture. Pour into buttered and floured cake pans. You may use 3 (8-inch) pans, or 2 (9-inch) pans, or a 13 x 9-inch pan (it will be very full). Bake at 350 degrees for 30 to 35 minutes. The oblong pan takes longer to bake, about 40 to 45 minutes.

BOILED ICING

2 cups sugar
1 cup water
Dash salt
2 egg whites
1 teaspoon vanilla

Combine sugar, water, and salt in saucepan; cook and stir over medium heat just until clear. Continue cooking without stirring until syrup spins a long thread when dropped from tip of spoon. Beat egg whites until soft peaks form. Add syrup until frosting will hold shape. Add vanilla.

This fudge recipe of Mother's was a challenge to make since I had to weigh and measure the ingredients and decide what degree a hot fire was. It takes a long time to make but is worth the effort. I made this and mailed it to John when he was gone for six weeks one winter hauling down South. He came home and I asked how he liked his candy, and he said he never received it. From wherever it was, eventually it was returned. It was still good!

BLACK WALNUT CREAM FUDGE

3 pounds sugar (6 cups)
2 pounds white corn syrup (3½ cups)
1½ pints sweet table cream (whipping cream or whole milk)
3 teaspoons vanilla
2½ pounds black walnuts, in shell (about 3 cups shelled)

Stir first 3 ingredients together in a large saucepan until thoroughly mixed. Set on a hot fire (medium heat) and stir constantly with a wooden spoon. Boil until a small portion forms a medium-soft ball in cold water. Remove from fire and stir until cool. Add nuts and vanilla and continue stirring until almost cold. Pour into a buttered pan. Makes 5 pounds fudge.

Since my mother's recipe made so much candy, I cut the portions down.

BLACK WALNUT CREAM FUDGE ADAPTED

2 cups sugar
¾ cup milk
⅓ cup white syrup
2 tablespoons butter
1 teaspoon vanilla
1 cup black walnuts

Cook sugar, milk, and white syrup until the soft ball stage. Remove from stove and add butter and vanilla. Cool to lukewarm then add walnuts. Beat until thick and creamy. Pour into buttered dish.

The cream pie is a recipe that Mother taught me to use. I love it as a filling for banana pudding. It also works as a great coconut cream pie.

CREAM PIE

¼ cup flour
½ cup sugar
¼ teaspoon salt
1½ cups milk
3 eggs, separated
2 tablespoons butter
½ teaspoon vanilla
6 tablespoons sugar
Baked 8-inch pie shell

Mix flour, ½ cup sugar, and salt in large skillet or pan; add milk and stir well. Cook over medium heat until thick and smooth, stirring constantly. Beat egg yolks well, stir in a little of the hot mixture and pour back into pan; cook on low for 2 minutes stirring constantly. Remove from heat and add butter and vanilla. Beat egg whites until light, and gradually beat in the 6 tablespoons sugar until stiff. Fold about ⅓ of the meringue into the cooled filling. Pour filling into cooled pie shell and spread remaining meringue over filling, so as to . touch the edges of the crust all around. Place in a 350 degree oven and bake 12 to 15 minutes or until golden brown. Cool before cutting.

COCONUT CREAM PIE

Use the cream pie recipe and fold ½ cup moist shredded coconut into the cooled filling just before folding in ⅓ of the meringue. Then sprinkle coconut on meringue before baking.

BANANA PUDDING

Use ½ of the meringue to fold into the cream pie. When cooled add alternate layers of pudding, bananas, and vanilla wafers. Top with the remainder of the meringue and bake in a moderate oven until golden brown.

I sometimes teach a course on Appalachian women to Elderhostel groups who come to Berea College. Ann Meinwald and her husband were in a class one year and bought a copy of my cookbook. We talked about foods from different places and our shared passion of collecting recipes. Ann gave me the following recipe for marmalade made a special way.

My husband and I travel quite a bit, love to go to England. I simply adored the English marmalade and bought jars to bring home with me. I kept trying to make marmalade to taste as good as the English kind. Finally I got something right and now I can say, gladly, that my recipe tastes better than any I ever bought in England, or anywhere else.

MEINWALD'S THREE-DAY, THREE-FRUIT MARMALADE

1 orange
1 grapefruit
1 lemon
(Or any variation you wish)

Day One: Remove pits, and slice very thin. Place in enamel-lined pot and add just enough water to cover the fruit. Leave on stove.
Day Two: Bring to a boil and boil for ½ hour.
Day Three: Measure fruit mixture and add equal amount of sugar. Cook for about 1 hour, skimming when necessary. Put in jar or glass and store in refrigerator.

Dorothy Miller, Berea, Kentucky

Dorothy Miller lived on Fee Street, and we were around the corner on High Street in Berea. She was a retired school administrator. Our landlady, Ruth Davis, and Dorothy were colleagues and friends and were often at each other's houses. Grover and Dorothy were good buddies, sharing a love of antiques. When More Than Moonshine *came out both Dorothy and Ruth bought copies. After that, we exchanged recipes and shared cooking tips from time to time. Dorothy gave Grover a few recipes and said someday I might want to use them in another cookbook. Dorothy passed away a year after that and her house was sold. I wish I had gotten other recipes from her.*

My Grandmother always used a hog's head and feet to make this dish, but I find that neck bones work just as well and are available in supermarkets.

HOG'S HEAD PUDDING

3 pounds pork neck bones or any scrap pork
1½ cups white cornmeal
½ teaspoon salt
½ teaspoon black pepper

Simmer pork in salted water to cover until meat is tender, about 1 hour. Drain, reserve broth. Measure broth, add water to make 4 cups. Return liquid to saucepan. Shred meat. Stir into broth with cornmeal, salt, and pepper. Bring to boil, stirring constantly. Cook and stir until thick enough to make a cross with a spoon, 5 to 10 minutes. Pour into a greased 9 x 5 x 3-inch pan. Cover and chill until firm. Unmold, cut into ½-inch slices, dust with flour. Brown in small amount of hot fat on both sides, about 10 minutes. Serve with warm syrup. (I like it better on hot buttered biscuits.)

FAMILY FRUIT CAKE

1½ pound pitted dates
1 pound whole candied cherries
1 pound candied pineapple
2 pounds pecans
4 eggs
2 teaspoons baking powder
2 cups all-purpose flour
1 cup sugar
½ teaspoon salt

Mix flour, baking powder, and salt. Add fruit. Beat eggs and add sugar. Pour over mixture and mix well. Add pecans. (You will have to use your hands to mix.) Place pan of water in bottom of oven. Line pans with wax paper; bake at 275 degrees 1¼ to 1½ hours.

This recipe is probably over two-hundred years old. It was handed down through our family for many years.

OLD-FASHIONED GINGERBREAD

½ cup butter
½ cup sugar
1 cup molasses
1 teaspoon salt
1 teaspoon cinnamon
1 teaspoon cloves
1 tablespoon ginger
1 tablespoon soda
2½ cups plain flour
2 eggs
1½ cups buttermilk

Cream butter and sugar together. Blend all other ingredients into creamed mixture. Grease and heat a 13 x 9-inch pan until real hot. Pour batter into pan and bake for 40 minutes in 350 degree oven.

Paul and Barbara Power, *Berea, Kentucky*

Barbara Power is head of the circulation department at the same library where I work. She is a great cook in her own right and often brings in cakes, pies, or cookies for coffee breaks. Needless to say these goodies are eagerly welcomed by the entire staff.

Paul is a retired faculty member from the English department. He is often involved in baking items for treats or celebrations by the library staff. Paul's specialty is making angel food cakes; whenever any of the staff are sick or in the hospital, one of his cakes arrives. He has other wonderful recipes also. Years ago he shared his recipe for bran muffins with me. This recipe is the best of many recipes I have for bran muffins.

This recipe was given to me by a friend several years ago. I have adapted it, changed the proportions of the dry ingredients, and experimented until it suited me.

PAUL POWER'S BRAN MUFFINS

3 cups whole wheat flour
2 cups white flour
5 teaspoons soda
2 cups sugar
Dash cinnamon
Pinch of freshly ground nutmeg
1 (15 oz.) box of raisin bran
4 eggs, beaten
1 cup oil
1 quart buttermilk
½ box raisins

Mix well
Let dough stand at least 24 hours before you bake any muffins. May be stored in refrigerator (will keep up to 6 weeks). When ready to bake, grease muffin tins and fill full. Bake for 20 minutes at 375 degrees.

Paul grates almost all of one small nutmeg when he bakes banana bread and also adds a small amount of allspice and a little cinnamon. I may or may not take time to grate a nutmeg.

BARBARA'S BANANA BREAD

2 cups sugar
½ cup shortening
2 eggs
3 cups flour
Pinch of salt
1½ teaspoons soda
8 to 10 tablespoons buttermilk
3 bananas, mashed

Mix in order given (add soda to buttermilk). Mix well and pour into either a loaf or Bundt pan. Bake at 350 degrees for 1 hour.

Charlotte Ross, *Boone, North Carolina*

I have known Appalachian scholar, folklorist, and storyteller, Charlotte Ross, for almost two decades. She and her husband, Carl Ross, taught at Appalachian State University in Boone, North Carolina, for a number of years. When I told her I was interviewing people for material to put in a cookbook, she began talking about her mother, grandmother, great-grandmother, and some of the old recipes which had been handed down in her family.

Sidney, I am sending you some old family recipes. My grandmother's mother, Fanny Ellanora Strawn Tyler, ca. 1871–1938, and her mother Nancy Black Strawn, ca. 1800–1928, who came into North Carolina before the Cherokees were removed in 1838, made the two following dishes. Strawn is a Welsh name. My first ancestor in America was Lancelot Strawn who settled in Bucks County, Pennsylvania, as a young man in the 1670s. His wife, Ruth Purcell of Scottish parentage, was the youngest person on William Penn's flagship. He (Penn) was her godfather. She was excommunicated from the Quaker

Sect when she married Lancelot Strawn. They had one son Jacob who married a Pennsylvania German girl and had sixteen children. I believe the first of these two recipes is from that Welsh and Scottish connection in early Pennsylvania—I found a lowland Scots recipe for Marlborough Pie which is similar—and the second recipe might be from the Pennsylvania German side of the family. Mama's apple custard pie was famous throughout North Georgia.

Nancy Black got this recipe and the one below from her mother-in-law, Elizabeth Strawn ca. 1803–1884. Elizabeth drew our farm in the 1832 Cherokee Land Lottery with her husband, Jackson Strawn, who had fought in the American Revolution. She was a young wife with two sons, one gun, one ox, one cow, and one axe, who came into the Murray County frontier in 1834—four years before the Indians left and was widowed soon afterward. One of the boys was mauled by a bear the day she staked-out our farm. She would have learned to cook in her western North Carolina childhood or in her young married days in upper South Carolina.

FANNY STRAWN'S APPLE CUSTARD PIE

3 eggs, separated, reserve whites for meringue
1 cup sugar, minus 4 tablespoons sugar to reserve for meringue
1 cup homemade applesauce, chunky
¼ cup milk
1 tablespoon flour
1 tablespoon butter
1 teaspoon vanilla

Cream 1 whole egg plus 2 egg yolks, sugar, butter, and flour. Add milk, applesauce, and vanilla. Pour into unbaked pie shell. Bake in 400 degree oven for 10 minutes. Reduce to 350 degrees for 30 minutes or until knife comes out clean. Make meringue from egg whites and 4 tablespoons sugar. Add meringue to finished pie and brown slowly until beads form.

My mother, Willie Sue Woody Tanksley, has reconstructed this recipe from memory. She helped her grandmother Fanny Strawn Tyler and her great-grandmother Nancy Black Strawn make it when she was young.

CORN DUMPLINGS AND TURNIP GREENS

After your greens start cooking, make up cornmeal dough (use enough flour to make dough stiff enough to roll out). Spread each dumpling out on a thin piece of cloth. Take leftover meat (almost always pork) and cut in small pieces. Add red and black pepper and spices to taste. Spread meat mixture on the dough. Now gather the cloth in and tie with a string. Drop dumplings into pot of greens. When greens are done, dumplings will be done. Remove dumplings from pot. Remove cloth. Place dumplings on dish and pour some pot liquor over them (not much). Dumplings are best made with ham hocks and cabbage.

Fanny cooked greens with ham bone and simply rolled her dumplings and dropped them in. Other women in the family lacked her deft touch and quick eye, so they had to use the cloth to duplicate her recipe.

This recipe never fails. Mama used this as the base for several of her custard pies.

GRANDMOTHER'S EGG CUSTARD

4 eggs
1 cup sugar
1½ cups milk
Nutmeg

Mix thoroughly. Bake in medium oven (325 to 350 degrees).

My grandmother, Clara Tyler Woody Swanson, had an unusually good Japanese fruit cake "receipt." She got it from her first husband, Lester Woody's family near Fort Loudon, Tennessee, about 1910.

JAPANESE FRUITCAKE

1 cup butter
2 cups sugar
3¼ cups flour
1 cup milk
4 eggs
1 teaspoon baking powder
1 teaspoon vanilla

Divide the batter. In one part put 1 teaspoon each of cinnamon and allspice, ½ teaspoon of cloves, and ¼ teaspoon finely chopped raisins. Bake this white cake mixture in two layers.

FILLING FOR CAKE

2 grated lemons, rind, juice, and pulp
1 coconut, grated
2 cups sugar
1 cup boiling water
2 teaspoons cornstarch

Mix everything except cornstarch. Boil. Add cornstarch. Cook until thick. Cover cake with white filling. Top with walnuts.

James Still, *Hindman, Kentucky*

James Still is a well-known writer and lecturer. He was the inspiration and advisor for More Than Moonshine, *so it was natural that I would want an interview with him for this book. A North Alabama native, he came to the mountains during the depression and has never lived anywhere else. Living alone, he has developed many quick shortcuts and unusual ways of cooking his food. I was never able to set up an interview with him, but we talked on an informal basis several times about food and cooking. He gave me the following recipes.*

STRAWBERRY SPREAD

3 tablespoons clear honey
2 tablespoons water
Fresh strawberries

Put ingredients in saucepan and cook until berries just begin to break. Good on toast or biscuits.

BEER BREAD

2 cups flour
1 teaspoon salt
8 to 10 tablespoons vegetable oil or shortening

Mix flour and salt. Add cooking oil and enough beer to make medium-thick dough. Grease and flour loaf pan and add dough. Bake at 350 to 400 degrees for 15 or 20 minutes, or until bread is done and nicely browned. Slice and serve hot.

Kimberly Sommerville, Louisville, Kentucky

Kimberly Sommerville entered Berea College as a freshman the same year my son Bruce Alan enrolled. They became friends and shared many things together, including a love for good food and cooking. Kimberly told me that since she was a young child she had dreamed of someday owning and operating a country inn. At a time when most teenage girls were reading Glamour, *and magazines like that, Kim subscribed to* Gourmet. *Both she and Bruce got degrees in hotel management and business.*

Kimberly was often at my house, both eating and cooking. After college her career took her away from Kentucky for awhile. She has managed restaurants and been the chief cook. Working up through the many stages of hotel management, she came to know that she loved cooking best of all. Currently, she is in training to become a chef. I asked her to share her most favorite recipes and she sent three.

These cookies are not too sweet. I made these in Germany when my aunt wouldn't let my cousin have sweets.

SESAME SEED COOKIES

¼ cup butter
1 cup brown sugar
1 egg
2 teaspoons vanilla
½ teaspoon baking soda
½ teaspoon salt
1 teaspoon baking powder
2 cups flour
1 cup sesame seeds

Cream butter, sugar, egg, and vanilla. Mix in remaining dry ingredients and shape into balls and flatten with sugared fork. Bake on greased baking sheet at 350 degrees for 10 to 15 minutes.

BUTTERMILK PIE

5 eggs
1½ sticks margarine, melted
¾ cup buttermilk
2 to 3 tablespoons flour
2½ cups sugar
½ teaspoon vanilla
Coconut (optional)

Blend sugar, flour, beaten eggs, vanilla, and buttermilk. Mix well. Pour into two deep-dish unbaked pie shells. Bake at 350 degrees for 45 minutes. Pie is good served plain, or sprinkled with coconut.

FRUIT COCKTAIL CAKE

2 eggs
1½ cups sugar
½ cup oil
1 teaspoon vanilla
2 cups flour
2 teaspoons soda
¼ teaspoon salt
1 can fruit cocktail
1 cup brown sugar
½ cup chopped nuts
1 cup coconut

Combine eggs, sugar, oil, and vanilla. Mix well. Sift flour, soda, and salt. Add alternately with fruit to creamed mixture. Beat well. Pour into ungreased 9 x 13 x 2-inch pan. Mix remaining ingredients and sprinkle on top of cake. Bake at 350 degrees for 35 to 45 minutes.

ICING

1 stick butter
½ cup evaporated milk
¾ cup sugar
½ cup nuts
½ cup coconut

Combine butter, milk, and sugar. Boil 2 minutes. Add nuts and coconut.

Michael Thompson, Berea, Kentucky

Michael Thompson is an associate in Impressions of Berea, an antique shop owned by Grover Farr. An extremely talented artist, Michael is also an herbalist and gourmet cook. It is always a treat to eat a meal which he has prepared.

My grandmother and grandfather Thompson owned a large farm when I was a child, and at harvest time fifteen to twenty men would be hired to work. Grandmother always cooked the noon meal for all the hands. For dessert, she often served the following recipe.

BUTTER ROLLS

3 cups milk
1½ cups water
1 cup sugar
1 teaspoon vanilla
Dash cinnamon (optional)

Heat above ingredients to near boiling point; set liquid aside but keep hot.

PASTRY

2 cups self-rising flour
¼ cup shortening
¾ cup buttermilk

Cut shortening into flour. Add buttermilk and stir just to mix. (You may prefer to use your own favorite biscuit recipe.) Roll out very thin and cut size you prefer or use a saucer.

FILLING

1½ tablespoons butter, softened
1 heaping tablespoon sugar

Mix and put filling on each circle of dough. Gather the edges up and seal in center (like you would an apple dumpling). Dust with cinnamon if desired. Pour hot liquid into a baking pan or dish, put rolls in liquid, and bake until top is golden brown. Serve warm. A delicious old-fashioned dessert.

PRUNE CAKE

Combine:
1 cup vegetable oil
2 cups sugar
3 eggs, beaten

Add:
2 cups flour
½ teaspoon cloves
½ teaspoon nutmeg
½ teaspoon cinnamon
½ teaspoon allspice
1 cup prunes
1 cup chopped nuts

TOPPING

1 cup sugar
½ cup buttermilk
½ teaspoon soda (add to buttermilk)
1 tablespoon dark Karo syrup
6 teaspoons butter

Combine oil, sugar, and eggs. Add flour, cloves, nutmeg, cinnamon, allspice, prunes, buttermilk, soda, vanilla, and nuts. Beat well. Pour into pan and bake at 350 degrees. Combine buttermilk and soda, syrup, and butter. Cook until it reaches the soft ball stage and then pour over cake. It will be thin.

This recipe is my grandmother Seals's recipe. It has been handed down in the family and is one of our most favorite cakes.

BLACK WALNUT BANANA CAKE

2 cups sugar
1 cup shortening
4 eggs
1 cup sour milk
2 teaspoons soda
¼ teaspoon salt
2 cups blackberry jam
¾ cup strawberry jam
2 bananas, mashed
½ of 8-ounce box dates
½ of 8-ounce box raisins
1 teaspoon allspice
2 teaspoons nutmeg
1 teaspoon cloves
3 heaping cups of flour
1 cup nuts

Mix ingredients in order as given. Roll dates and raisins in flour before adding to mixture. Grease and flour a very large tube pan or 3 loaf pans. Bake at 350 degrees about 2 hours. Set a pan of water underneath for steam.

GRANNY'S POUND CAKE

1 pound butter, at room temperature
3 cups sugar
3 cups sifted flour
10 eggs, at room temperature
1 teaspoon vanilla (if desired)

Cream butter and sugar well. Add eggs and flour alternately. Grease and flour tube pan, pour in batter, and bake for 1½ hours at 325 degrees.

RUMAKI

½ pound chicken livers, cut to bite size
1 pound bacon, slices cut in half
1 bottle soy sauce
Pinch of nutmeg
1 teaspoon ginger
2 cloves garlic, crushed
2 bay leaves

Make marinade with soy sauce, ginger, garlic, nutmeg, and bay leaves. Wrap liver with ½ slice of bacon. Secure with toothpick. Marinate overnight. Broil or bake at 400 degrees for 15 minutes. Then turn and cook an additional 5 to 7 minutes.

One year, some friends generously shared their abundant crop of yellow tomatoes, and I fixed them every way I could think to serve them. I decided to create a good soup and came up with the following recipe.

YELLOW TOMATO SOUP

10 to 12 medium yellow tomatoes, steamed and quartered
8 to 10 cloves, whole
3 bay leaves
3 to 5 cloves garlic
1 medium onion, quartered
A good pinch of cayenne pepper
Hot sauce to taste
½ teaspoon basil (or more to taste)
¾ teaspoon salt
2 tablespoons sugar

Put all ingredients in big saucepan or kettle and bring to slow boil. Cook for
10 minutes or until tomatoes are tender. Run through sieve. Serve garnished
with croutons or a dab of yogurt. Spices may be adjusted to suit personal
taste.

Elizabeth Watts, *Pleasant Ridge, Tennessee*

*A New England native, Miss Watts came into the mountains when she
was just out of college. She rode in as far as she could on a train, she says,
then rode horseback through the hills and valleys until she arrived at the
Hindman Settlement School in Knott County. She worked in various
capacities; when I knew her years later she was the director of the center.
When she retired from there she lived in Berea for several years. She gave
me a couple of recipes one day after we'd spent time together reminiscing
about the early days in the mountains. She is one hundred years old.*

A woman named Rosemary Stovall gave this recipe to me. It is the best chocolate cake you will ever eat.

CRAZY CHOCOLATE CAKE

1½ cups flour
1 teaspoon soda
½ teaspoon salt
1 cup sugar
3 heaping tablespoons cocoa
5 tablespoons light cooking oil (such as sunflower or safflower)
1 tablespoon vinegar
1 teaspoon vanilla
1 cup cold water

Sift flour, soda, and salt directly into an 8- or 9-inch square pan. Stir in sugar and cocoa. Blend well, and make three "wells" in the mixture. In one well, pour vegetable oil, in the second, put vinegar, and in the last the vanilla. Add cold water over all. Stir but don't beat, with a fork. Bake at 350 degrees for 20 to 30 minutes, testing for doneness with a toothpick. Dust with powdered sugar to serve, or use this easy icing:

ICING

In a saucepan combine 1 square bitter chocolate, ½ stick butter or margarine, ¼ cup milk, and 1 cup sugar. Bring to a boil, then cook a minute, stirring all the while. Cool. Then beat a few minutes and pour on top of cake.

My Recipes
Recipes from Stoney Fork and Berea, Kentucky

WHEN I *am in pain or feel that the world is closing in on me, one thing will make me feel better and that is to cook food like my mother did when we lived on Stoney Fork in southeastern Kentucky. Green beans, fried corn, biscuits, fried chicken and gravy, mashed potatoes, baked ham, homemade pickles, soup beans with ham hock—these are foods that I can take out and savor in memory even if I am not prepared to cook foods like that for my next meal. Usually though, I do cook at least one dish like my mother did.*

CORN PUDDING

2 cups fresh corn
2 tablespoons flour
1 teaspoon salt
3 tablespoons butter
3 whole eggs
2 tablespoons sugar
1 cup milk

Blend butter, sugar, flour, and salt. Add eggs, beating well. Stir in corn and milk. Pour into buttered dish and bake 45 minutes at 325 degrees. Stir once halfway through cooking.

GREEN BEANS

1 ham bone
1 quart water
1 onion
½ to 1-inch red pepper pod
2 pounds green beans
1 tablespoon sugar
1 teaspoon monosodium glutamate (MSG), if desired
1 teaspoon salt

Put ham bone in a pot or pressure cooker with the water, onion, and pepper. Boil about 2 hours or cook 45 minutes in the pressure cooker until all the essence has been extracted. Strain. Refrigerate or freeze stock until ready to use. If the bone was not too bare, this should season 2 pounds of beans.

Put beans in stock with sugar and MSG. Simmer, covered, about 1 hour. Add salt and cook uncovered, 30 minutes longer. Or put beans in pressure cooker with stock and cook for 15 to 20 minutes. Drain beans; leftover stock or juice is good over biscuits or corn bread.

Our whole family loved mashed potatoes, especially when served with chicken gravy. Freshly dug, peeled potatoes cooked until soft, seasoned with butter, salt, and pepper, simply makes the most delicious addition to any meal.

MASHED POTATOES

Cook amount of potatoes needed for people to be served. When potatoes are done, drain and mash with a potato masher until all lumps are gone. Quickly stir in salt and pepper to taste and add butter and a little cream or whole milk (use your judgment according to how many potatoes you cooked) and stir until potatoes are white and fluffy. Serve hot.

FRIED CORN

6 ears of corn
4 tablespoons bacon fat
2 tablespoons butter
1 tablespoon sugar
½ cup water
1 teaspoon salt
Freshly ground pepper to taste

If the kernels are small, cut the corn once; if they are large, cut the ends of the kernels, then cut a second time. Finish by scraping with the back of the knife to get every bit of pulp and milk (the more of this the better the corn will be).

Let the butter and bacon fat get hot in a heavy skillet. Put the corn in, add sugar, and cook over medium heat, without stirring, until corn begins to brown on the bottom. Use a spatula and turn the corn, scraping up all of the good brown part that adheres to the skillet. Add water, salt, and plenty of pepper. Cover and let steam for 8 to 10 minutes or until corn is done and water has evaporated. Again scrape the skillet and stir the browned part into the corn. Always cook corn as soon as it is husked and cut from the cob. If more convenient, it may be fried ahead of time and reheated by adding a little water and steaming. Serves 4.

POTATO DUMPLINGS

1 pint mashed potatoes
1 egg
Enough flour to thicken

Add egg to potatoes and work in flour. Roll into balls the size of walnuts and drop into boiling water; cook for 20 minutes. Serve with gravy.

BAKED APPLES AND SAUSAGE

Fill a casserole half full with cored and quartered apples. Sprinkle with sugar and a little cinnamon. Place pork sausage balls on top and bake until apples and sausage are done.

BAKED BEANS, MOUNTAIN STYLE

2 tablespoons brown sugar, firmly packed
2 teaspoons flour
2 teaspoons prepared mustard
⅓ can evaporated milk
1 (8 oz.) can pork and beans
1 frankfurter, optional

Thoroughly mix sugar and flour in small pan. Stir in mustard, then evaporated milk. Add beans and mix well. Cover, cook over low heat 5 minutes. Stir, then cover, cook 5 minutes longer. Serves 2.

Option: Frankfurter, sliced thin, may be added to the beans.

STONEY FORK SWEET POTATOES

3 cups cooked sweet potatoes, mashed
1 tablespoon butter
2 tablespoons molasses

Put potatoes in greased casserole. Boil together molasses and butter for 7 minutes. Pour over sweet potatoes and bake at 350 degrees until browned a little bit.

SISTER'S SWEET POTATO SOUFFLE

1 can sweet potatoes, cooked and mashed
⅓ cup hot skim milk
1 tablespoon butter or margarine
2 teaspoons grated lemon rind
½ teaspoon salt
Pepper, if desired
2 egg whites, stiffly beaten

Add hot milk and margarine to sweet potatoes and beat until fluffy. Add lemon rind, salt, and pepper. Fold in stiffly beaten egg whites. Bake in greased casserole in 400 degree oven for 35 minutes. Serves 4.

In 1983, Cheryl Southerland, a college student from Spring City, Tennessee, bought a copy of *More Than Moonshine* and, later, came to meet me. She gave me this recipe.

ASPARAGUS ON BREAD

Asparagus
Bread
Mushrooms
American cheese, grated
Parmesan cheese

Place asparagus on bread. Put mushrooms, American cheese, and Parmesan cheese on top. Heat until cheese is bubbly; turn up heat and brown a little.

CREAMED MEATBALLS

1 pound ground beef
½ cup water
¼ cup bread crumbs
2 tablespoons minced onions
1 tablespoon minced parsley
1 egg, slightly beaten
Shortening
1 can cream of mushroom soup

Add water, bread crumbs, onions, parsley, and egg to ground beef. Shape into sixteen meatballs. Put shortening into skillet and brown meatballs. Pour off fat and add soup. Cover and simmer 15 minutes, stirring often. Serves 4.

HEALTHY CARROT MEAT LOAVES

3 pounds lean ground beef
3 cups shredded carrots
1½ cups chopped onions
1½ cups dry bread crumbs
1½ cups tomato juice
3 eggs
1½ teaspoons salt
1 teaspoon ginger
1 teaspoon curry powder

Mix all ingredients. Divide in thirds. Shape each third into a loaf in a large baking pan or press gently into three 9 x 5-inch loaf pans. Bake in a preheated 350 degree oven for 1 hour or until done as desired. If serving immediately, let stand 10 minutes before slicing; or cool, wrap, and refrigerate up to 3 days; or freeze up to 2 months. Makes 3 loaves, 4 servings each.

In microwave oven, cook 1 meat loaf at a time in a shallow dish on high for 12 minutes, turning dish once halfway through cooking. Let stand five minutes before slicing and serving.

Sometime after World War II grocers stocked their shelves with Spam and other canned luncheon meats. Mother and my aunts were glad to get them because they were relatively cheap and had a different taste. The women were creative in finding a variety of ways to serve these types of foods.

SPAM AND GREEN BEAN CASSEROLE

¼ cup butter
2 medium onions, sliced
½ cup flour
¼ teaspoon pepper
1⅔ cups evaporated milk
1 pound can cut green beans
12 ounce can luncheon meat
1 tablespoon butter
1 slice bread

Melt ¼ cup butter in saucepan over low heat. Add onions and cook until tender. Remove from heat, stir in flour, pepper, and milk. Add green beans with their liquid. Return to heat and cook, stirring occasionally, until thickened. Cut lunch meat into ½-inch strips, add to bean mixture. Turn into a well-greased 1½ quart baking dish. Melt 1 tablespoon butter and remove from heat. Pull bread into small crumbs, add to butter, mixing lightly with fork. Spread buttered crumbs evenly over top of meat mixture in baking dish. Bake in preheated 350 degree oven until crumbs are browned, about 15 minutes. Serves 6.

BAKED TOMATOES

12 large tomatoes
Bread crumbs
1 egg yolk
Pepper and salt to taste
Butter

Peel tomatoes then cut slits in their sides. Stuff the slits with a mixture of bread crumbs, egg yolk, pepper, salt, and butter. Place tomatoes in a shallow pan and bake until done. Pour a little drawn butter over them and serve hot.

SALMON CASSEROLE

1 large can salmon
½ cup bread crumbs
½ cup chopped celery
3 egg yolks, slightly beaten
1 tablespoon lemon juice
3 egg whites
½ cup melted butter
2 slices of bread, cubed

Mix salmon, bread crumbs, celery, egg yolks, and lemon juice. Beat egg whites stiff and fold into above mixture. Mix melted butter with cubed bread and place on top. Set casserole in pan of water and bake 50 minutes at 350 degrees.

CREAM BISCUITS

2 cups flour
2 teaspoons baking powder
1 teaspoon salt
8 tablespoons shortening
1 cup cream

Preheat oven to 450 degrees. Sift flour with baking powder and salt. Cut in shortening until texture resembles coarse cornmeal. Add the cream and work into dough, kneading several times. Roll out dough on floured board until it is about ½ inch thick. Cut into biscuits and place in lightly greased pan. Bake 10 to 15 minutes. Makes 10 to 12 medium biscuits.

At home we didn't have cakes and pies very often because of the expense in making them. One time that we could count on though was at Christmastime. Mother made a yellow cake with meringue frosting which she called our Christmas cake. She also made dried apple stack cakes. The following is a basic recipe for jam cake which I've had for some time. Following that is another version.

CHRISTMAS JAM CAKE

6 eggs
1 cup melted butter
3 cups sifted flour
4 tablespoons buttermilk
1 teaspoon baking soda
1 cup blackberry jam
1 cup walnuts or pecans
1 cup raisins
2 cups brown sugar
2 teaspoons cinnamon
2 teaspoons allspice
2 teaspoons nutmeg
Bourbon whiskey, optional

Mix eggs with melted butter, brown sugar and jam. Add flour, cinnamon, allspice, and nutmeg. Fold in walnuts or pecans. Bake in 9-inch tube pan greased with 1 part flour to 2 parts butter rubbed together. Bake at 325 degrees for 1½ to 2 hours. Let cool 5 minutes then turn out on rack. Add bourbon, if desired, to bottom of cake by piercing bottom with fork.

ANOTHER CHRISTMAS JAM CAKE

1 cup butter or margarine, softened
1 cup sugar
1 cup firmly packed brown sugar
2 eggs
4 cups sifted cake flour
1 tablespoon cocoa
2 teaspoons soda
½ teaspoon salt
1 teaspoon ground cinnamon
1 teaspoon ground cloves
1 teaspoon ground nutmeg
2 cups buttermilk
1 cup blackberry jam
1 cup chopped nuts
1 cup raisins

Cream butter and sugars in large mixing bowl. Add eggs, beating well. Sift together flour, cocoa, soda, salt, and spices and add to creamed mixture alternately with buttermilk. Beat well after each addition. Stir in jam, nuts, and raisins. Pour batter into 3 well-greased and floured 9-inch cake pans. Bake at 325 degrees for 45 minutes or until cake tests done. Cool in pans 10 minutes; remove cake to a wire rack and cool completely. Frost cake as desired.

AUNT HONEY'S PUMPKIN PIE

1½ cups canned or cooked pumpkin
½ cup honey (use a little more if desired for sweetness)
½ teaspoon cinnamon
½ teaspoon vanilla
½ teaspoon salt
2 eggs, slightly beaten
1 cup evaporated milk
1 unbaked pie shell

Combine pumpkin, honey, cinnamon, vanilla, and salt. Add eggs and milk. Pour mixture into pie shell and bake at 425 degrees for 40 to 45 minutes.

POOR MAN'S CAKE

1 cup sugar
1 egg
2 level tablespoons butter or margarine
1 cup milk
2 scant cups flour
3 level teaspoonsful baking powder
1 teaspoon vanilla or other extract
⅓ level teaspoon salt

Beat the egg and sugar together until light; add the milk, melted butter and extract. Sift flour, salt, and baking powder and add the liquid mixture and beat well. Bake about 45 minutes at 325 to 350 degrees or until tests done.

GRANNY BROCK'S PECAN CAKE

3 sticks butter, softened
2 cups sugar
6 eggs
½ cup maple syrup
¼ cup bourbon
4 cups flour
1 teaspoon baking powder
½ cup orange peel (optional)
1 pound pecans
1 whole clove, shaved
1 pound box golden raisins

Cream butter and sugar, then add eggs, beating after each one. Mix maple syrup and bourbon together. Sift flour and baking powder and add to creamed mixture alternately with syrup mixture. Stir in orange peel, pecans, shaved clove, and raisins. Mix well. Grease tube pan with mixture of 1 part flour to 2 parts shortening, rubbed together. Pour into pan and bake at 250 degrees for 3 hours.

ROSE-COLORED CAKE

1 cup sugar
½ cup shortening
1 teaspoon soda
1 can tomato soup
2 cups flour
1 teaspoon baking powder
1 teaspoon cinnamon
1 teaspoon ground cloves
½ teaspoon salt
½ to 1 cup nuts
1 cup raisins (optional)

Cream sugar and shortening. Dissolve soda in tomato soup. Sift flour, baking powder, cinnamon, ground cloves, and salt together. Combine and add nuts and raisins. Bake in slow oven for 1 hour. Cover with cream cheese frosting.

Note: To make this cake quickly, use a package of 2-layer spice cake mix with a can of tomato soup, ½ cup water, and 2 eggs. Mix all ingredients and bake according to package directions.

FROSTING

1 package cream cheese
1½ cups powdered sugar
1 teaspoon vanilla
Dash of nutmeg

Mix above ingredients well and frost cake while slightly warm.

HUCKLEBERRY CAKES

½ cup butter and lard mixed
1 cup sugar
2 eggs, separated
½ cup milk
2 cups flour
1½ level teaspoons baking powder
½ teaspoon nutmeg
½ teaspoon cinnamon
Pinch of salt
2 cups huckleberries

Beat the shortening and sugar until creamy. Add the egg yolks and milk. Sift flour, baking powder, spices, and salt together, and add to creamed mixture. Fold in the huckleberries and stiffly beaten egg whites lightly and gently. Bake in greased shallow pan.

Mother's blackberry cobbler was much simpler than the following recipe. We had lots of blackberry cobblers in the summertime when berries were in season. Canned blackberries never tasted as good, we thought, therefore we had few if any cobblers during the fall, winter, and spring months. She always made up dough as though for biscuits. If she had cream she would use it to moisten the dough. She pinched off wads of dough and rolled each in her hands. Then she would stretch the dough out into an oval shape and put it on top of the fruit or berries. Sometimes she sprinkled sugar over the top to make it browner. We always ate every crumb of her cobblers.

BLACKBERRY COBBLER

4 cups fresh, or 2 (16 oz.) packages frozen and thawed blackberries
¾ cup sugar
3 tablespoons all-purpose flour
1½ cups water
1 tablespoon lemon juice
Crust (recipe follows)
2 tablespoons melted butter or margarine
Cream and sugar (optional)

Place berries in a lightly greased 2-quart baking dish. Combine sugar and flour; add water and lemon juice, mixing well. Pour syrup over berries. Bake at 350 degrees about 15 minutes while preparing crust.

CRUST

1¾ cups all-purpose flour
2 to 3 tablespoons sugar
2 teaspoons baking powder
1 teaspoon salt
¼ cup shortening
6 tablespoons whipping cream
6 tablespoons buttermilk or sour milk

Combine flour, sugar, baking powder, and salt. Cut in shortening until mixture resembles coarse crumbs. Stir in whipping cream and buttermilk. Knead dough 4 or 5 times. Roll to about ¼ inch thickness on a lightly floured surface. Cut dough to fit baking dish. Place crust over hot berries; brush with butter. Bake at 425 degrees for 20 to 30 minutes or until crust is golden brown. Serve warm with cream and sugar, if desired. Serves 8.

OLD-FASHIONED CHERRY PIE

4 cups pitted cherries
1½ cups sugar
3 tablespoons flour
3 tablespoons cornstarch

Mix cherries, sugar, flour, and cornstarch. Pour into 9½-inch pie dish lined with pastry and cover with top crust in which openings have been cut. Moisten the edge of crust; press together, flute, and trim. Bake in hot oven (425 degrees) for 40 to 45 minutes.

   Note: If canned cherries are used, decrease the sugar to 1 cup, and the cornstarch and flour to 2 tablespoons each. Drain juice from cherries, add flour and cornstarch to juice (there should be at least 1½ cups of juice; if not, add water for the correct measuring). Cook over slow heat until thickened, then add cherries. Cool slightly before putting into pastry.

   My great-grandmother, Granny Brock, Granny's daughter Susie (my grandmother) both used dried fruit for fried pies and other kinds of pies instead of canned fruit during the winter months.

DRIED FRUIT PIE

Dried fruit
Dough for 2-crust pie
Sugar to taste

Wash the fruit and soak it overnight. Next morning stew it until it is nearly done, and sweeten to taste. Put the cold fruit into a pastry-lined pie pan, with plenty of juice. Place top crust over fruit and seal the edges. Put slits in the top crust so steam can escape. Place in a 350 degree oven and bake until crust is brown.

Helpful Hints, Old and New

• To make a pecan pie without nuts, substitute crushed cornflakes. They will rise to the top the same as nuts and give a delicious flavor and crunchy surface.

• To make a quick frosting, boil a potato, mash it, and add powdered sugar and vanilla.

• Stir half a package of chocolate chips into your 7-minute frosting while it is still hot. It will turn out creamy and taste wonderful.

• If you dust a little flour on top of a cake before icing, the icing will not run off.

• Add a little sugar to the milk in fried cakes, fritters, etc., because this prevents the cakes from absorbing the fat in the frying.

• Shortly before you take cupcakes from oven, place a marshmallow on each for the frosting.

• The gelatin around canned ham is marvelous for flavoring green beans. Add enough water to gelatin to cover beans and cook as directed. Excellent also for cooking navy beans, black-eyed peas, or kale greens.

• If you add a little bit of baking powder to potatoes just before you cream them, they will be fluffier.

• Rub a little cooking oil around the top of the cooking pot and it won't boil over.

• A little butter added to cooking rice will keep it from boiling over.

• Start fresh vegetables to cooking in cold water. This helps vegetables to hold their flavor.

• Baking soda on a damp cloth will remove grime and grease from glass on oven door.

• A mixture of half hot vinegar and half salt rubbed on copper or brass will clean and polish.

• He or she who has baked a good batch of bread has done a good day's work.
• Cold tea is good for your hair. Use it as a dressing every day and a head of glossy, luxuriant hair will result. Black tea is best.
• Sprinkle salt over your carpets just before sweeping and it will brighten colors and prevent moths.
• When painting a room, cut an onion in half and leave the pieces standing all night. It will destroy the odor of paint.
• To renovate a dust mop, put a large tablespoonful of concentrated lye in an old pail half full of boiling water and let boil in it. Rinse several times. Mop will be as good as new.
• Household ammonia will take out scorch stains.
• It is said that if you pour 2 tablespoons castor oil around the roots of your Christmas cactus in October it will bloom in December!
• Plant Narcissus bulbs on Armistice day and they will bloom on Christmas day.
• How to make a Rosebud Quilt: Take 16,450 pieces cut the size of a milk bottle cap. Turn edges carefully and gather toward center, fasten securely. Result should be size of a tiny forget-me-not blossom. Join seven of these blossoms, six surrounding a center one, all a different print but harmonious as one small rose. Continue until you have sufficient roses for a good-sized bedspread. Fasten roses securely together and you have one of the most beautiful bed coverings imaginable.

Index

259